EXTREME RÉSUMÉ MAKEOVER

THE ULTIMATE GUIDE TO RENOVATING YOUR RÉSUMÉ

PLUS SECTIONS ON COVER LETTERS, THANK-YOU NOTES, AND ELECTRONIC RÉSUMÉS

CINDY KENKEL
Department of Marketing and Management
Northwest Missouri State University

McGraw-Hill
Irwin

Boston   Burr Ridge, IL   Dubuque, IA   Madison, WI   New York   San Francisco   St. Louis
Bangkok   Bogotá   Caracas   Kuala Lumpur   Lisbon   London   Madrid   Mexico City
Milan   Montreal   New Delhi   Santiago   Seoul   Singapore   Sydney   Taipei   Toronto

The McGraw·Hill Companies

McGraw-Hill
Irwin

EXTREME RÉSUMÉ MAKEOVER:
THE ULTIMATE GUIDE TO RENOVATING YOUR RÉSUMÉ

Published by McGraw-Hill/Irwin, a business unit of The McGraw-Hill Companies, Inc., 1221
Avenue of the Americas, New York, NY, 10020. Copyright © 2007 by The McGraw-Hill
Companies, Inc. All rights reserved. No part of this publication may be reproduced or distributed
in any form or by any means, or stored in a database or retrieval system, without the prior written
consent of The McGraw-Hill Companies, Inc., including, but not limited to, in any network or
other electronic storage or transmission, or broadcast for distance learning.

Some ancillaries, including electronic and print components, may not be available to customers
outside the United States.

This book is printed on acid-free paper.

1 2 3 4 5 6 7 8 9 0 QPD/QPD 0 9 8 7 6 5

ISBN-13:   978-0-07-351182-5
ISBN-10:   0-07-351182-X

Editorial director: *John E. Biernat*
Publisher: *Linda Schreiber*
Sponsoring editor: *Doug Hughes*
Editorial assistant: *Peter Vanaria*
Marketing manager: *Keari Bedford*
Media producer: *Benjamin Curless*
Project manager: *Jim Labeots*
Lead production supervisor: *Michael R. McCormick*
Coordinator freelance design: *Artemio Ortiz Jr.*
Cover design: *George Kokkonas*
Typeface: *10/12 Times New Roman*
Compositor: *GTS – New Delhi, India Campus*
Printer: *Quebecor World Dubuque Inc.*

Library of Congress Cataloging-in-Publication Data

Kenkel, Cindy S.
    Extreme résumé makeover: the ultimate guide to renovating your résumé /
Cindy S. Kenkel.—1st ed.
        p. cm.
    Includes index.
    ISBN-13: 978-0-07-351182-5 (alk. paper)
    ISBN-10: 0-07-351182-X (alk. paper)
    1. Résumés (Employment) 2. College students—Employment. 3. College
graduates—Employment. I. Title.
HF5383.K416 2007
650.14'4—dc22

                                                              2005044405

www.mhhe.com

PREFACE

Preparing a résumé and cover letter can be an overwhelming challenge for college students. Most have had only minimal experience putting together such important documents. All too often, the final products end up selling the student short. While several exceptional books feature samples of professional résumés, very few feature quality samples targeted exclusively for students seeking an internship or their first professional position.

Trading Spaces . . . While You Were Out . . . Extreme Makeover . . . What Not to Wear . . . The Date Patrol. Our nation is obsessed with makeovers, so I have decided to play along. The *before* and *after* sample résumés will provide students with concrete visual examples to use as models for their final product.

I've reviewed résumés from students who attend institutions around the country, and I rarely find versions that are as good as they could be. Readers who first glance at the samples may even think the *before* samples look ready to go. In reality, the *after* versions will greatly enhance a student's ability to secure an interview that will eventually lead to a job.

Of course, no résumé should leave home without a date, so I have also included the résumé's partner—the cover letter. For years, this document took backstage because it was, to be honest, boring. This book features samples using the "two-column" or "T-format," which demonstrates exceptional targeting to the employer's needs. Letters using this format can be easily adapted to fit each position.

I have blended knowledge gained from spending 12 years as a human resource manager, one year directing a highly successful outplacement program (we won an award from the governor of Missouri for our effort), and eight years of teaching college business communication to create this user-friendly, do-it-in-a-weekend guide to creating résumés and cover letters that really work.

ACKNOWLEDGMENTS

This book was possible only through the help of hardworking, talented students in my courses who were willing to write and rewrite their résumés too many times to count. One of the things that separates this book from others on the market is that the résumés and letters were written by real students instead of professional résumé writers. All of the students agreed to allow their documents to be published; their names and identification information have been changed.

Without the help of two truly exceptional students, Kerra Siefering and Kari Frerking, the layout and finishing touches would not have happened. Dr. Mona Casady, from Southwest Missouri State University, also provided exceptional assistance early in the book's creation. The Career Services department at Northwest Missouri State University also worked diligently with my students to help perfect their résumés.

Keeping with the theme of featuring student work, Lindsay Little, a student in our mass communications department, created the professional cover page first used for this book. Adam Jones, Anvar Gabidouline, and Joni Adkins all helped develop the step-by-step process covered in the electronic résumé section. Together we have prepared a foolproof list of directions for even novice computer users. Katie Knobbe and Holly Eschenbauch often pitched in, researching and helping to fine-tune sections of the book.

A special thanks to the "go to" person in our department, Ann Clark, for her efforts to make this project happen.

The following students agreed to have their real names mentioned in the acknowledgments: Debbie Thurman, Stephanie Meints, Darcy Hall, Jennifer Cooper Jensen, Monica Fine, Lindsey Frerking, Michelle Eischeid, Kari Frerking, Sachie Handa, Amy Andrews, Daniel Jeppersen, Nick Talone, Jamie Tindall, Amanda Duncan, Chris Provorse, Brett Simons, Andrea Tappmeyer, Elizabeth Carver, Keri Crawford, Sarah Colter, Emily Dettmar, Rachel Hildebrand, Lisa Crater, Astra Haney, Katy Laswell, Jamie Longenecker, Chris Motsinger, Joe and Kelli Quinlan, Julie Stith, Skylar Rolf, Anthony Kreikemeir, Praveena Kandasami, Lauri Whittington, Jennifer Smith, Sarah Cole, Brad Woodard, Renae Miller, Kelvin Parker, Brooke Boynton, April Miller, Traci Eggers, Jamie Smith, Catherine Skeen, David Clements, Jill Culley, Vincent Giambrone, Ryan Vansickle, Julie Bennett, Adam Jones, Sara Bornholdt, and Corey Wilson.

My deepest gratitude also goes out to the McGraw-Hill staff who have worked hard to ensure a product students will really use has been crafted.

My husband, Phil, and children, Hailey and Tyler, demonstrated exceptional patience during both the writing and editing process. All three inspire me daily as they pursue their passions with vigor and devotion.

Thank you to all the reviewers who provided suggestions that truly enhanced the book:

JoAnna Downey
Corinthian Colleges, Inc.

Karine Blackett
National American University Online

Peggy S. Schlechter
National American University

Marianne Auten
Paradise Valley Community College

Janet Bayless
Remington College

Kristen Aust
Bryant and Stratton College

Michelle Adams
Bryant and Stratton College

Ellen Carte
Valley College of Technology

Sharron Dillon
Branford Hall Career Institute

Carol Jo Reitz
Allentown Business School

Dr. Mona J. Cassidy
Southwest Missouri State University

Kelly Edmondson
Central Missouri State University

Donna Campbell
Gonzaga University

Ronald Weber
Florida Metropolitan University

Dr. Kimme Nuckles
Baker College

Donald E. Crews
Southwest Georgia Technical College

Kristin E. Wissinger
Penn Commercial, Inc.

Justin P. Barclay
International Institute of the Americas

Julie R. Cervantes
Everest College

Dr. Joan Neal-Mansfield
Central Missouri State University

Sharon Occhipinti
Florida Metropolitan University

Marilyn Joseph
Florida Metropolitan University

Susan K. Rumans
Remington College

Christian Blum
Bryant and Stratton College

Sharon L. Youngue
Art Institute of Phoenix

Clara Loftin
Kerr Business College

BRIEF CONTENTS

TABLE OF CONTENTS

PART THREE

THANK-YOU NOTES

PART ONE 1

Résumés

CHAPTER ONE

Getting Started

Your first step is to review several résumés to get a feel for what they will entail. Choose samples closely related to your field of study. As you review these, highlight information that relates to you. Now is *not* the time to get dazzled by the layout; just focus on content and information.

The first hurdle you face is deciding what to include on your résumé. No hard and fast rules in this arena exist, but some excellent guidelines are available. After helping over 1,800 students prepare résumés over the last few years, I have determined that one of the major struggles you face is separating content from format. Using the résumé worksheet has virtually eliminated this obstacle. Even if you have already started your résumé, it is critical that you fill out the worksheet prior to worrying about format.

Put everything on your worksheet. Skip sections if they do not pertain to you, but be careful not to filter at this point. You are brainstorming, not evaluating. Often, asking a parent, friend, or roommate to help you with this exercise yields more complete results. Keep this worksheet readily available because it is an excellent tool to use as you fill out applications, prepare for employment interviews, and tweak your résumé to fit each position for which you are applying. After reading through the "Frequently Asked Questions" section, you will be ready to fill out your worksheet and get started.

■ FREQUENTLY ASKED QUESTIONS

Do I need an objective?

Experts really disagree on this issue. You will hear some who adamantly believe you need one and others who are just lukewarm about objectives. As long as your cover letter clearly identifies your target, you *officially* do not need one. My suggestion is to include either a specifically targeted objective or a summary section to open your résumé.

During your parents' era, we used flowery objectives that really added nothing to the document. Today these would yield the gag reflex from most hiring professionals. Stay away from this type of objective. My first résumé objective went something like this: "To effectively utilize the skills and knowledge I have obtained studying management to improve the productivity at your organization." Now, including the title or department (that often is a keyword) in which you are interested is enough for an objective.

What is a summary? Is it the same thing as a profile?

Yes, a summary and a profile are the same thing. Using a preview of your material perfectly targeted to the employer's position or organization will most effectively utilize the 30 to 45 seconds that hiring professionals will spend initially reviewing your résumé. It sets the tone and quickly identifies you as a serious contender for a position or organization. See Andy Paxton's (pp. 86–87) and Angelo Rodriquez's résumés (pp. 88–89).

Why do you want me to fill out the profile section of the worksheet last?

I have included this section early in your worksheet because it belongs early in the résumé. However, I have asked you to complete it after you have filled out the rest of the worksheet because it is a summary. This section of your worksheet needs to fit each job you are targeting based on the skills you have to offer. I once had a student working on a group paper ask for input on his section (the conclusion). When I asked to review the body of the paper so that I could help, he was stumped; he had not actually written the paper yet. Needless to say, I could not offer any feedback at this stage of the game. You will be in a much better position to prepare your profile after you have completed the rest of the worksheet.

Why does the education section ask about coursework and projects?

Often your work or leadership experience is less critical to a position than the information you are obtaining while pursuing your degree. Let's think about this. Students often devote a line of their résumé to a one-time community service activity, such as walking dogs for a local humane society, but leave off a semester-long project. Including a brief description of a major project gives you an opportunity to demonstrate teamwork, problem solving, written and oral communication skills, and the ability to apply what you are learning. Incorporating keywords into your résumé will be discussed later.

When do I include my grade point average (GPA)?

Most experts agree on this rule. The magic number is a B average or 3.0 on a 4.0 scale. A few tricks are available if you do not have a B average. If you have close to 30 hours in your major, you can use your major GPA; but you will need to clearly label it as such. Since it takes some students longer than others to adapt to college, using your junior/senior GPA is another option. Again, your junior/senior GPA needs to be clearly noted as a junior/senior GPA.

As a hiring professional, I always was willing to overlook a GPA of lower than a 3.0 if a student spent significant time working or participating in campus athletics or activities. Including a statement within your education section that highlights this participation is critical. For example, "Work 25–30 hours per week to finance education" or "Education is partially financed through athletic scholarship" will help make up for a GPA that doesn't make the 3.0 cutoff.

Does a study-abroad experience belong on my résumé?

Absolutely. Study abroad usually works best as a bullet under education. Clearly identify the dates and where you went or plan to go. If you completed an internship while studying internationally, you will also discuss the internship in a separate internship or work experience section.

Which positions do I include in my work experience section?

It depends. At this point in your career, you typically will include all jobs you have held. If you already had an internship or highly relevant position, you will devote more space to these descriptions. Focus should be on skills the employer will need (teamwork, communication and interpersonal skills, leadership skills, problem solving, time management, and work ethic). Knowing that a student has worked each summer since high school in a variety of settings is as important to many hiring professionals as an internship or professional position. Showing any increased responsibility or promotions from summer to summer also is important.

Do I need a separate section for my internship?

Using a separate section for an internship is one way to help it stand out. You probably want to do this if it isn't your most recent position so that your jobs will still be listed in reverse chronological order. Keenan Joiner did this on his résumé on pp. 103–104. A separate section also works well if you have experienced more than one internship (which is becoming more and more common).

What do you mean by focusing on accomplishment and transferable skills? It is hard to accomplish a lot working in a fast-food restaurant.

Try to include at least one accomplishment for each position: for instance, "Chosen employee of the month, Never missed a day of work, or Demonstrated initiative by taking on management responsibilities." Verbs such as *awarded, bolstered, earned, overhauled, prevented, spearheaded, transformed, tripled,* and *won* work well. See the special category of verbs designed for highlighting one of your accomplishments found in Appendix A.

Including a discussion of transferable skills really helps the employer see how your work experience has impacted you. For example, if you worked as a server in a restaurant, you might end your description with a statement such as "Enhanced ability to multitask in a fast-paced environment." In a fast-food establishment you might have "Developed an appreciation for working with team members from diverse backgrounds." As a secretary you might have "Demonstrated ability to pay attention to details." Being asked to return to a job over breaks and the next year or to accept a full-time position upon graduation definitely is something to include. Verbs that work especially well for highlighting transferable skills are *achieved, attained, developed, encountered, enhanced, fine-tuned, mastered, refined,* and *strengthened.*

What do you mean by "action verbs"?
Numerous lists of action verbs are available for you to reference as you prepare your work and leadership experience sections. Starting each sentence of your description with an action verb keeps your résumé active rather than passive. Ideally, you limit your use of an action verb to one per job or activity. Use present tense for jobs you currently have and past tense for jobs you previously had. Refer often to the list of verbs in Appendix A.

Instead of generic action verbs such as "assisted" or "helped," which can be unclear, use concrete action verbs. I can say "assisted you in preparing a résumé," but what does this mean? It could mean "checked it for spelling and grammatical errors." Or it could mean "coached you during one-on-one sessions to ensure that you included critical information targeted to an employer's position specifications in a highly professional document." The last example provides concrete versus generic details.

What are keywords and how do I make sure I have them included in my résumé?
Employers are looking for an individual with specific skills and experience to fit different positions. The easiest way for employers to screen résumés is to identify those who are the best match for each position by identifying the skills or attributes they are seeking through the use of keywords. This often is done through counting (manually or with software) the number of keywords found on a résumé. Imagine the person responsible for screening applicants searching their database for these keywords; as in most search engines, the document, file, or Web site that has the most "hits" or "matches" will get the most attention or a higher ranking.

Keywords are not the same thing as action verbs; instead, they are nouns and noun phrases that are position or industry specific. While you'll often read about using keywords in a discussion of scannable résumés, it is just as important to include them in your traditional résumé. Keywords are most powerful if included in a profile or summary of skills *and* sprinkled throughout your document. The qualifications listed early in an ad often carry the most weight, so be sure you address these areas.

The best place to determine keywords for a particular position is to have a copy of the position description nearby. Keywords can be found on an employer's Web site, in a vacancy announcement, or in a newspaper advertisement. You can use reference material such as *The Dictionary of Occupational Titles* or *Occupational Outlook Handbook,* available online. Web sites such as www.salary.com provide position titles and position descriptions that often are packed with keywords. The table below reflects the most common categories of keywords and a few examples particularly relevant to college students.

Certifications	CPR/First-Aid, Customer Service Certificate, MOUS, Certified Ergonomic Specialist
Computer languages	COBOL, FrontPage, JAVA
Foreign languages	Spanish, French, Japanese, Chinese, study abroad
Industry jargon or buzzwords	Business plan development, total quality management (TQM), customer service, front of the house, business ethics, sales
Personality traits/ transferable skills	accountable, adaptable, ambitious, budget conscious, computer literate, creative, dependable, detail oriented, easy to get along with, ethical, focused, hardworking, honest, loyal, persuasive, persistent, problem solver, reliable, resourceful, results oriented, self-starter, team builder, team player, troubleshooter

Position titles	Advisor, Assistant, Coach, Computer Tutor, Consultant, Counselor, Customer Service Clerk, Help Desk, Intern, Internship, Judicial Liaison, Lab Assistant, Liaison, Manager, Office Assistant, Peer Advisor, Peer Counselor, Paralegal, Practicum, President, Project Manager, Teaching Assistant, Sales Representative, Secretary, Supervisor, Team Leader, Teller, Treasurer, Vice President, Volunteer
Prestigious companies	McGraw-Hill, Hallmark, Georgia-Pacific, Rubbermaid Corporation, Fortune 500, Allied Health
Schools	Harvard, Yale, Northwest Missouri State University
Honor societies	Delta Mu Delta (business), Delta Kappa Psi (freshman) Honor Society, Phi Eta Sigma (freshman), Mortar Board, Delta Tau Alpha (agriculture society), Pi Omega Pi (business education), Order of Omega (Greek honor society), Kappa Omicron Nu (family and consumer science), Psi Chi (psychology)
Products/Industries	Automotive, financial, disposable diapers, soft goods, insurance, health care, banking, allied health
Software programs/ Computer skills	Microsoft Office, Word, PowerPoint, Excel, Publisher Access, Internet Explorer, Netscape Navigator, Outlook, QuickBooks Pro, Quicken Deluxe, PhotoShop, computer-aided design (CAD), AOL Press, QuarkXPress, computer guru
Technical skills	typing 70 wpm, file and database management, project management, team building, computer literacy, cold-calling, accounting, customer service, trained, payroll, accounts receivable/payable, selection, security, public relations, invoices, upscale cliental, negotiations, page layout, value-added selling, client presentations
Types of degrees/ Courses	AA, AS, BS, BA, MA, MBA, MS
	Certificate in Dental Technology, Certified Legal Assistant (CLA), Certified Athletic Trainer (ATC)
	Accounting, Integrated Software, Managerial Communication, Business Communication, Finance, International Business, Sales

Although the list isn't all inclusive, it should get you thinking. A list of keywords for each field of study also is included prior to each résumé sample section.

<u>I am having a tough time describing my work and leadership experience. Do you have any tips?</u>

Have someone help you clearly articulate what you mean for this section. Get a fellow student to take notes while you simply tell your friend what you did at your job. If something you say is not clear, your friend should ask you to clarify. Do not worry about making your position description sound extravagant. Just say what you did. Then go back and substitute action verbs at the beginning of each duty.

<u>What do you mean by "quantify"?</u>

After you've written basic descriptions of your duties, review and quantify or qualify anywhere you can. Instead of saying "Wrote news releases," say, "Wrote five news releases each week." Anytime you can be specific and use numbers, do so.

Generic	Quantified
Planned activities	Planned daily activities, including games and outings for 20 students
Assisted clients over the phone	Assisted approximately 50 claimants per day with questions regarding their claim over the phone
Organize and sell retail inventory	Organize and sell retail inventory of $6,000 per year
Perform routine office duties	Selected by VP of Finance to assist in coordination of $15.1 million budget of Garret-Strong renovation

<u>Do I really need to include a section called computer skills?</u>

Most students include computer skills somewhere within their résumé because they are common keywords. Use a separate section if your major deals exclusively with computers or if your skills are superior to most of your peers. You can also include this information if you need more words to fill up the page. Columns work well for this type of section. If your skills are basic (Microsoft: Word, Excel, PowerPoint, and Internet search engines), you probably will include it as a bullet in your education section. Be sure to include any programs used in work experience descriptions.

Which leadership and campus involvement activities do I use?
The worksheet is separated into columns so that you can see how these activities should be grouped. Include all organizations that are related to your major or field of study. If you have not joined any of these organizations yet, get moving. Join early in your educational career so that you will be ready for a leadership position prior to graduation.

Include social organizations if you have been involved as either a leader or committee representative. Just paying dues and showing up for the social activities is not enough. Include any activities that demonstrate talent or teamwork skills, such as the debate team, band, athletics, or intramural activities.

Many experts caution against including religious and political activities because they could lead to discrimination. If you have developed skills particularly relevant to the position at your church or working for a political association, you may still want to include them. You will have to weigh the benefit of highlighting these skills with the understanding that it may lead to discrimination.

Where do I list my community service activities?
Community-oriented activities can be listed in your leadership or campus involvement section or put in their own section if they are impressive enough. Mention the amount of time you spend at these activities if it is significant. For instance, "Walked dogs at the local humane society once a week for the last three years."

If I don't really have any honors or achievements, what do I put here?
Just leave it blank. If you have just a few scholarships, honor societies, or honor roll listings, include the information within your education section. Freshmen, sophomores, and first semester juniors can include *select* accomplishments from high school. High school accomplishments should be included only if they are significant and relevant. If you were in Future Business Leaders of America in high school and competed or placed at a state level competition, add this. Although being elected homecoming attendant is an impressive accomplishment, it isn't related to your future career, so leave it off.

I have lots of honors and achievements. Do I include them all?
Put them all on the worksheet, because you can choose which ones to include when you are formatting your résumé. You would be amazed at how many you can include if you leave off dates and put them in a two- or three-column format. Similar to the computer skills section, honors and achievements should be logically grouped.

Do my references' names belong on my résumé?
Usually not. A separate page will be used to list your references and their contact information. At the top of this page, use the same format as you've used in your résumé. If, after preparing your résumé, it ends up being over one page, you can use the bottom of the second page to note your references. When including references, be sure the layout is attractive. It often works well to lay them out in columns; all of the information needs to be included for each reference.

References by Permission:

Ms. Cindy Kenkel
Management Instructor/Advisor
Northwest Missouri State University
800 University Drive
Maryville, MO 64468
(660) 562-1652
Ckenkel@mail.nwmissouri.edu

Dr. Jimmy Walker
Marketing Professor
Wayne State College
600 College Drive
Wayne, NE 52501
(402) 562-1861
JWalker@mail.waynestate.edu

Dr. Ronald Platt
Director of Statistics
KC Stats
1103 West 108th Street
Overland Park, KS 66219
(913) 469-8886
KCstats@asde.net

Ms. Della Owens
Guidance Counselor
Maryville Middle School
8210 School Way
Maryville, MO 64468
(660) 582-6875
Dowens@k12.edu

You do not need to place a statement on the bottom of the first page indicating that your references are available upon request, because everyone knows you will provide this information if it is requested. Rarely a statement "References will be provided upon Request" may be used to fill up the page or to provide a look of closure. If you have a portfolio of your work available, you should add a statement indicating that one is available (i.e., "Portfolio Available").

How do I know whom to include as a reference?
Human resource professionals are leery of personal references. You are safest using any current or previous supervisors or employers, academic advisors, faculty, coaches, and campus organization sponsors as references.

It is important that you get advance approval from people you are asking to serve as a reference. Asking prospective references if they know you well enough to provide a positive reference helps give them a way out if they don't feel comfortable. Providing references with a copy of your résumé will allow them to provide relevant information when prospective employers call.

Résumé Worksheet

CONTACT INFORMATION
Name

School Address   Phone

Permanent Address   Phone

E-mail (must be professional; school address is OK)

OBJECTIVE— _____
Position title or department   Employer's name

PROFILE—Refer to job advertisement, Web site, or personal conversation with the organization

Top 4–6 requirements of the position	Brief description of how you meet these—complete this column after you've filled out the rest of the worksheet.

EDUCATION
Spell out your Degree Name (MBA, MS, BS, BA, AA, Diploma) _____
Major(s) _____ Minor(s) _____
When will you receive this degree? Month _____ Year _____

_____
College or University Name   City, State

Major GPA _____   Overall GPA _____
___ Number of semesters on Dean's List (3.5–3.99)   ___ Number of semesters on President's List (4.0)
___ Hours worked per week while attending school
___ Percent of education you pay for with scholarships or work
___ Number of scholarships you have; list them

___ Check if you have any of the following: ACT of 30 or higher, 80 percent or higher on standardized test such as an academic profile that shows you are a good student, 80 percent or higher on a standardized test that verifies you have mastered material in your major such as a Major Field Achievement Test (MFAT). You might check your college catalog to get the exact name of the test you took.

___ Check if you have knowledge of any foreign languages.
List languages and degree of competence (basic understanding, familiar with, proficient, fluent).

___ Check if you have or plan to study abroad (when and where _____).
Briefly describe the experience.

List 6–12 courses you will have taken prior to starting the job that are directly related to it.

MAJOR PROJECTS

Provide a brief description of your major projects (team projects, senior projects, simulations). Refer to the keywords section appropriate for your major prior to completing this section.

1.

2.

3.

4.

5.

6.

7.

LEADERSHIP/CAMPUS INVOLVEMENT (Include any offices within the group.)

Major related clubs	Social (Greek, religious, etc.)	Talent required (athletic, drama, etc.)	Community oriented	Other

KEY SKILLS (Provide a two or three word explanation of any that apply.)

Excellent Communication Skills (written, oral, or both)

Honesty/Integrity

Interpersonal Skills (gets along well with others)

Initiative/Motivation

Leadership

Strong Work Ethic (hardworking)

Analytical/Reasoning

Good at Solving Problems

Flexible

Creative

Tactful/Aware of Business Etiquette

Fun to Work With

Solid Grasp of Field Knowledge (grades or standardized test)

Willing to Relocate

WORK EXPERIENCE (List and describe ALL internships and positions.)

_____	_____,	_____	____ - ____
Title	Employer's Name	Location	Month/yr. Month/yr.

Overview of the type of company, products, or service, and your role.

List your most important duties; each should start with an action verb (quantify if possible).

Describe your major accomplishments; refer to the accomplishments category on the action verbs list.

Discuss any transferable skills you obtained; refer to the transferable skills category on the action verbs list.

_____   _____, _____ _____ - _____
Title   Employer's Name   Location   Month/yr. Month/yr.

Overview of the type of company, products, or service, and your role.

List your most important duties; each should start with an action verb (quantify if possible).

Describe your major accomplishments; refer to the accomplishments category on the action verbs list.

Discuss any transferable skills you obtained; refer to the transferable skills category on the action verbs list.

_____   _____, _____ _____ - _____
Title   Employer's Name   Location   Month/yr. Month/yr.

Overview of the type of company, products, or service, and your role.

List your most important duties; each should start with an action verb (quantify if possible).

Describe your major accomplishments; refer to the accomplishments category on the action verbs list.

Discuss any transferable skills you obtained; refer to the transferable skills category on the action verbs list.

_____   _____, _____ _____ - _____
Title   Employer's Name   Location   Month/yr. Month/yr.

Overview of the type of company, products, or service, and your role.

List your most important duties; each should start with an action verb (quantify if possible).

Describe your major accomplishments; refer to the accomplishments category on the action verbs list.

Discuss any transferable skills you obtained; refer to the transferable skills category on the action verbs list.

			,		-
Title		Employer's Name	Location		Month/yr. Month/yr.

Overview of the type of company, products, or service, and your role.

List your most important duties; each should start with an action verb (quantify if possible).

Describe your major accomplishments; refer to the accomplishments category on the action verbs list.

Discuss any transferable skills you obtained; refer to the transferable skills category on the action verbs list.

Add another sheet if you have more jobs.

COMPUTER SKILLS (List all programs—applications and databases, programming languages, and operating systems with which you are familiar.)

Proficient with		Familiar with

HONORS/ACCOMPLISHMENTS (List honor societies, scholarships, special awards, etc. If you are a junior or senior, list only those you've received in college.)

Choosing a Format

After your worksheet is complete, you are ready to plan the format. Your résumé has to make an exceptional first impression. It needs to WOW the reviewer. It needs to scream professionalism. One way to ensure this *does not* happen is to use a résumé template found in your favorite word processing programs. Résumé templates are disliked by hiring professionals because they demonstrate a lack of creativity. The other major weakness of templates is that they don't allow you enough flexibility.

Instead of using a preformatted template, review the *before* and *after* samples again, but focus on format this time. Choose a format you like and model your résumé to match it. One of the easiest ways to follow a format is to access the model you like from the CD included with your book.

Since résumé writing is more of an art than a science, the formatting tips I offer below are based on my preferences. While I do not have concrete evidence that they always work, anecdotal evidence suggests they are effective. Students often are complimented on their résumé by interviewers. After studying five or six of the *before* and *after* samples, you no doubt will start to see why these formats work.

Should I use both my present and permanent address?
It depends; this immediately flags you as a recent graduate so some experts suggest using only one address. Always use your present address. Include your permanent address if you are applying for a position in or near your hometown or will be returning to your permanent address for an extended break from school.

I have two e-mail addresses. Which one should I use?
The most important element here is to use a professional address. Your school account is acceptable, but often a more personal account is used when you will be graduating soon. Remove the hyperlink on the address after placing it in your résumé so that the text is black. You remove the hyperlink by right-clicking on the address and choosing Remove Hyperlink. Never use your employer's e-mail address on your résumé.

How much white space (blank areas that separate information) do I need?
Effective use of white space is critical. Margins usually are set at one inch on all sides, although occasionally reducing to 0.8 inch if it is necessary. The white space needs to be distributed throughout the résumé. Odd chunks on the top, bottom, or on one of the sides are distracting. Ample space needs to be used to clearly separate sections of the résumé. Having items right on top of each other looks too crowded. Have at least some space between descriptions of your jobs.

Use only one space after each period in a paragraph.

I like the column look but can't figure out how to get the bullets.
Using columns for your coursework, computer skills, honors, activities, and accomplishments effectively utilizes space and looks professional. An easy way to use columns and bulleted items is to type the list with the bullets straight down the left side of the résumé, highlight the information, then choose the column button from the task bar, and experiment with two or three columns.

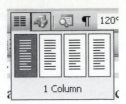

<u>Which font style and what size should I use?</u>
Your name needs to really stand out. Use a font large enough for this to happen. The name should never play second stage to your contact information.

Section headings stand out more if they are bold. Several fonts I especially like for section headings are:

Times New Roman 12

Times New Roman 14

Bookman Old Style 12

Rockwell 12

Wide Latin 12

My font of choice for the majority of your text is Arial. It is easy to read and you can go down to size 9 if necessary. Times New Roman 10 is more difficult to read than Arial 9.

Times New Roman 9	Arial 9
Times New Roman 10	Arial 10
Times New Roman 11	Arial 11

Quite often when a student is convinced he or she cannot get the information to fit on one page, it is due to the font being too large.

<u>Should I use bullets or a paragraph to describe my work experience?</u>
Either works well depending on how much information you have to include. Bulleted items are easier to read. If you do use bullets, be sure you use a professional style rather than an asterisk (*) or hyphen (-). Stick to using only one or two types of bullets with the text spaced 0.15 to 0.25 away from the bullet. Avoid an overbulleted résumé. If you look down the left side and everything has a bullet, you have overdone it. If you've tried bullets but run out of room, switch to a paragraph format.

If you use the paragraph format, you may want to use a bullet at the end of the paragraph to emphasize your accomplishment or transferable skill. Darbi Thurman did this on her résumé on pp. 101–102.

<u>Should I use fancy lines, text boxes, page borders, and shading?</u>
Some type of fancy line under your name offers an exceptional way to help it stand out. I think text boxes offer an excellent way to clearly identify section headings, but not all experts agree. Students often draw text boxes with the line draw feature, but I strongly suggest that you use the features found under the Format menu if you are using Microsoft Word so that the lines or boxes adjust if you change your margins.

For a border around a section heading:

1. Select Format, then Borders and Shading; select Borders.

2. Click on Box and then pick your style of line and set the width (usually leave it on its default).

3. Under Preview be sure all the appropriate lines are selected so they will form a rectangle.

4. Apply to paragraph and click OK.

To shade the area within a bordered section heading:

1. Select Format, then Borders and Shading; select Shading.
2. Click on a gray shading color; I usually recommend 20 percent or less.
3. Apply to paragraph and then click OK.

Objective

OBJECTIVE

OBJECTIVE

Keep any shading fairly light.

OBJECTIVE
_____

Page borders work well if the rest of your design is simple. See Lynette Johnson's example on pp. 94–95.

How do I get it all to fit on one page?

1. Check your word count. You should be able to get 400, even 500, words on one page. Look at Angelo Rodriquez's after example on pp. 88–89, which includes 520 words.
2. Check your margins. They should be set at 0.8 to 1 inch on all four sides. You can even go to 0.6 on the top if you need to.
3. Check to see your font used on the majority of your text is legible yet as small as possible. My favorite is Arial 9, 9.5, or 10. Headings should, however, be _at least_ one size bigger than the rest of your text.
4. Switch to a paragraph format if you are using bullets.
5. Use columns for sections such as coursework, computer skills, honors, and activities. You probably can omit the dates here.
6. Minimize the space a blank line after a section heading is taking by reducing the font size in that section. This is simply done by moving your cursor to the blank line and reducing the font size to 4 or 5. You will probably have to type the font size into the box because it won't show up as an option on the drop-down feature.

I'd like to add a really unique element to my résumé. Do you have any suggestions?
Tasteful and appropriate clip art is shown on Kimberly Thurman and Dai-Hua Tung's examples (pp. 54–55, 99), specialty bullets are found on several of the cover letters (pp. 118–141), and quotations on Kara Fray's (pp. 24–25) can all really spice up a résumé. If you choose to use any of these design elements, they need to fit both your personality and the occupation you are targeting. In the past year or two these design elements (which once were considered too flamboyant) are now becoming acceptable. Most important is that the document remains professional.

How do I know when my résumé is good enough to send?
Résumés have to be completely error free. If you've followed the tips in this guide, you should be well on your way to having an exceptional résumé. Refer to the Résumé Checklist found in Appendix B to ensure that you are pulling all of the tips together. It is ideal to allow a faculty member and someone in a career department on your campus to also review your document. A word of caution: Résumé writing is an art; it isn't a science. People will have different opinions about your résumé; ask for clarification and reasoning behind suggestions if they differ from the views found in this book.

Before and After Résumé Examples

■ ACCOUNTING, ECONOMICS, AND FINANCE

Amanda McGinness—Accounting
Accounting firms are looking for students with impeccable style. They need to clearly demonstrate their ability to pay attention to detail, show high academic achievement, and emphasize an internship or related work experience.

Shelby Jones—Accounting/Finance
Shelby freshened up her résumé by expanding on almost every area. She went out of her way to inform the employer of the skills she possesses that fit the finance field.

Kara Fray—Finance
Kara's résumé spent a day at the spa shedding some of its dates. While her extensive experience and campus involvement could have warranted a two-page version, Kara wanted to stick to one page.

Keywords for Accounting, Economics, and Finance

Positions—Sought, Held, or Reported To			
• Accounting Manager	• Chief Financial Officer	• Intern	• Tax Finance Manager
• Analyst	• Comptroller	• Internship	• Team Leader
• Assistant	• Controller	• Loan Officer	• Teller
• Attorney/Lawyer	• Director Corporate	• Management Trainee	• Treasurer
• Auditor	• Director of Finance	Intern—worked closely	• Vice President of
• Chief Economic	• Economist	with the CFO	Accounting, Economics,
Officer	• Financial Advisor	• Manager	or Finance
	• Financial Analyst	• Office Assistant	

Industry Jargon			
• Administer surveys • Advise policy makers • Asset/liability management • Audit controls • Audits • Balance sheet • Banking/credit union • Bookkeeping • Budget • Budget deficits • Business cycles • Business to business • Capital budgeting • Capital campaign • Cash management • Collect and analyze data • Conduct research • Consulting • Cost analysis	• Cost reduction • Cost-benefit analysis • Credit and collections • Database design • Debt financing • Develop forecasts • Devise methods and procedures • Employee Stock Ownership Plan (ESOP) • Employment levels • Energy costs • Environmental and worker safety regulations • Equity financing • Exchange rates • Financial analysis • Financial planning • Financial statements	• Foreign exchange • General ledger • Inflation • Interest rates • Internal controls • Investing • Investor relations • IPO • Job costing • Leveraged buy out (LBO) • Model/business case development • Monitor economic trends • Payable/receivable • Portfolio • Posting • Preparing reports • Presenting economic and statistical analysis • Project management	• Quantitative analysis • Return on assets (ROA) • Return on equity (ROE) • Return on investment (ROI) • Risk analysis • Risk assessments • Risk management • Sampling techniques • Security pricing and analysis • Stock/bond valuations • Strategic planning • Taxes • Venture capital • Welfare policies

Degrees and Certifications	Personality Traits	Computer Skills	Professional Associations
• Bachelor of Science in Accounting • Bachelor of Science in Economics • Bachelor of Science in Finance • Certified Financial Manager (CFM) • Certified Financial Planner (CFP) • Certified Public Accountant (CPA) • Charted Financial Analyst (CFA) • CMA • Customer Service Certificate • Masters in Accounting or Management Information Systems • Masters of Business Administration, emphasis in Accounting • Public Track/Private Track	• Accountable • Analytical • Budget conscious • Dependable • Detail oriented • Ethical/honest • Leadership abilities • Precise • Problem solver • Professional • Project oriented • Quick learner • Resourceful • Responsible • Team player • Troubleshooter • Work well under pressure	• Microsoft Access • Microsoft Excel • Microsoft Outlook • Microsoft PowerPoint • Microsoft Publisher • Microsoft Word • Oracle • Peachtree • PeopleSoft • QuickBooks • Quicken • Turbo Tax • Windows OS • WordPerfect	• Accounting Society/ IMA • American Economics Association (AEA) • American Finance Association (AFA) • Beta Alpha Psi • Financial Management Association (FMA) • Omicron Delta Epsilon • Pi Beta Alpha • Students In Free Enterprise (SIFE) • Volunteer Income Tax Association (VITA)

Amanda McGinness

Present Address:
214 S. Stewart St., Apt. 12
Murfreesboro, TN 87649
(945) 592-5555
amcginness@hotmail.com

Stick to one address so not quickly identified as new graduate

Permanent Address:
410 E. Buckeye Rd.
Deerfield, TN 68492
(706) 745-8888

OBJECTIVE   To obtain a spring internship as an auditor or tax accountant at a public accounting firm

EDUCATION   **Middle Tennessee State**, Murfreesboro, Tennessee. Graduation date April 2005. Bachelor of Science in Public Accounting. 3.95 grade point average on 4.0 scale.

Grade point doesn't stick out

WORK EXPERIENCE   **Intern for Sales Secretary II/Staff Assistant**. May 2003 through August 2003. Oilers State Industries, Deerfield, Tennessee.
- Designed drawings and demo chairs databases in Microsoft Access
- Trained the sales department to use the drawings database
- Logged and entered all orders in orders database and prepared monthly reports on direct orders
- Monitored all sales orders for past due orders and problem orders
- Updated procedures for sales department
- Provided customer service

White space concentrated on sides

Intern for Accounting Clerk I. May 2002 through August 2002
Oilers State Industries, Deerfield, Tennessee.
- Prepared inmate payroll and purchasing reports monthly
- Trained new accounting clerk
- Coded sales orders and payments to be processed
- Matched purchase orders with their receivers and invoices
- Updated accounts receivable and payable files and the company's contacts
- Assisted buyer with purchasing products and work production orders

HONORS AND ACTIVITIES
- Presidential Scholars List (Fall 2001 through present)
- Phi Eta Sigma Honor Society (Spring 2002 through present)
- Mortar Board "Top 10 Sophomore Award" (Spring 2003)
- Delta Mu Delta Business Honor Society (Fall 2003 through present)
  - Secretary (Spring 2004 through present)
- Alpha Chi Society (Fall 2003 through present)
- Mortar Board (Spring 2004 through present)
  - Treasurer (Spring 2004 through present)
- Accounting Society (Fall 2001 through present)
  - Vice President (Spring 2004 through present)
- Professional Business Assembly (Fall 2001 through present)
  - Professional Chair (Fall 2002 through Spring 2003)
  - Membership Chair (Fall 2002 through Spring 2004)
- Students in Free Enterprise (Fall 2003 through present)
- Sigma Sigma Sigma Sorority (Fall 2002 through present)
  - Sisterhood Chair (Spring 2003 through Fall 2003)
  - Mini Float Homecoming Chair (Spring 2003 through Fall 2003)
  - Robbie Page Philanthropy Chair (Spring 2004 through present)
- Middle Tennessee State University Greek Week 2003
  - Activities Committee (Spring 2003)
- Middle Tennessee State University Homecoming 2003
  - Public Relation Committee (Spring 2003 through Fall 2003)
- Middle Tennessee State University Women's Golf Club (Spring 2003)

Dates distracting

Needs to be logically grouped

COMPUTER SKILLS   QuickBooks Pro, Great Plains Dynamics 6.0, Microsoft Word, Microsoft Excel, Microsoft Access, Microsoft Outlook, Microsoft Publisher, Microsoft Power Point, Microsoft Photo Imager, Quicken Deluxe, Print Shop Pro, Web pages, Internet Explorer, NCR System.

Word Count: 459

Amanda McGinness

Address: 214 S. Stewart St., Apt. 12, Murfreesboro, TN 87649 Ph: (945) 592-5555
E-mail Address: amcginness@hotmail.com

OBJECTIVE

To obtain a spring internship as a tax accountant at KPMG LLP.

Concrete objective

EDUCATION

- Masters of Business Administration Degree, August 2006
  - ~ Middle Tennessee State, Murfreesboro, Tennessee   GPA 4.0/4.0
- Bachelor of Science in Public Accounting, May 2005
  - ~ Middle Tennessee State, Murfreesboro, Tennessee   GPA 3.95/

Descriptive and detailed explanations

RELATED JOB EXPERIENCE

Tyler, Perky & Sampson, LLC   **Windrow, Tennessee**   **Spring 2005**

- Intern
  Prepared individual tax returns involving schedule C business owners, itemized deductions and multiple state returns on Prosystems fx. Gathered missing information from clients to prepare their tax return. Prepared corporate, partnership, and individual extensions. Assisted eight associates with various tax assignments and research projects. Experienced the busy tax season firsthand.

Oilers State Industries   **Deerfield, Tennessee**   **Summer 2002 & 2003**

- Intern for Sales Secretary II/Staff Assistant
  Designed drawings and demo chairs databases in Microsoft Access. Trained the sales department to use the drawings database. Logged and entered all orders in database and prepared monthly reports on direct orders. Monitored all sales orders for past-due and problem orders. Provided customer service. Developed more advanced computer skills along with training and presentation skills.
- Intern for Accounting Clerk I
  Prepared inmate payroll and purchasing reports monthly. Trained new accounting clerk. Coded sales orders and payments to be processed. Matched purchase orders with their receivers and invoices. Assisted buyer with purchasing products and work production orders. Observed firsthand how accounting practices were used in real businesses.

HONORS & ACTIVITIES

- Accounting Society
  Vice President & Tutor
- Professional Business Assembly
  Membership & Professional Chair
- Mortar Board "Top 10 Sophomore Award" (10 Sophomores)
- Alpha Chi Honor Society (Top 10% of Juniors and Seniors)
- Delta Mu Delta Business Honor Society Secretary
- Mortar Board (Senior Honor Society) Treasurer

- Phi Eta Sigma Honor Society (Freshman with 3.5 GPA)
- Tennessee Society of CPA's—Northwest Chapter Scholarship Recipient
- Sigma Sigma Sigma Sorority
  Mini Float Homecoming Chair
  Overall Homecoming Representative
  Robbie Page Philanthropy Chair
  Sisterhood Chair
- Greek Week (Activities Committee)
- Homecoming (Public Relations Committee)
- Women's Golf Club

COMPUTER SKILLS

- Accounting Software: ProSystems fx, QuickBooks Pro, Great Plains Dynamics 6.0, Quicken Deluxe
- Other Software: Microsoft Office, Internet Explorer, Banner Internet Database

Word Count: 445

Shelby Jones

310 West Harris Street
Norwalk, CA 64488
841-944-3711 (cell phone)

Objective: To secure an internship with a progressive company.

Education: Downey High School, Downey, CA, graduate, 2003
California State University–Fullerton, 30 hours
Wentworth Junior College, Lexington, CA, 6 hours, summer
Western State College, St. Joseph, CA, 6 hours, summer

Skills/Abilities: Dependable, honest, quick learner, customer service skills, written
and oral communication skills, computer knowledge, leadership
skills

Work Experience: Sunshine Greenhouse, Norwalk, CA, 2000–2004
- Retail Assistant
- Work well with customers and co-workers
Hyvee Supermarket, Downey, CA, 2004–to current
- Service Meat/Seafood Clerk

**Student
Organizations**:   National Dean's List
National Collegiate Scholars
Delta Kappa Psi National Honor Society
Future Career and Community Leaders of America
Future Business Leaders of America

Awards/Honors: Academic Honor Roll
Maintained a GPA of 3.5 or higher
National Honor Society all 4 years in high school

This résumé
has a <u>long</u>
way to go

Word Count: 139

SHELBY JONES

Local Address
301 W. Harris St.
Norwalk, CA 64488
Mobile: 841-944-3711

E-mail: sjones001@hotmail.com

Permanent Address
5555 Walter St.
Downey, California 65836
Home: 841-449-2068

OBJECTIVE

To secure a summer internship in the Finance Department for the Federal Reserve Bank

EDUCATION

Bachelor of Science, Double Major: Corporate Finance/Private Accounting   May 2007
California State University at Fullerton   GPA 3.75/4.00
   ❖ Classes to be completed by Summer 2006:
      ~ Fundamentals of Finance   ~ Managerial Communications
      ~ Intermediate Accounting I   ~ Computers and Info Tech
      ~ Investment Management   ~ Financial Institution
   ❖ Work 15–20 hours weekly while attending school full-time

WORK EXPERIENCE

Hy-Vee Supermarket   Downey, California   August 2004–Present
Service Meat/Seafood Clerk
Ensure speedy service while preparing food, serving customers, taking meat/seafood orders, and cleaning the meat department. Required to multitask in a fast-paced environment. Responsible for cleaning and closing the Service Meat Department.

Sunshine Greenhouse   Norwalk, California   March 2000–August 2004
Retail Assistant
Accurately handled up to $200 in money transactions daily. Listened to customers' needs and directed them to the type of plants that would work best in landscaping their homes and businesses. Worked with a team of 10 ensuring plants remained healthy and ready to sell. Demonstrated creativity by making floral arrangements for the City Market each week.

COMPUTER SKILLS

Microsoft Software: Word, Excel, Publisher, PowerPoint, Access, Works, Photo Editor
Other: Internet Explorer, e-mail

HONORS AND ACTIVITIES

~ National Dean's List
~ National Society of Collegiate Scholars
~ Delta Kappa Psi National Honor Society (freshman)

~ Academic Honor Roll–GPA 3.5/4.0 (all semesters)
~ Academic Excellence Scholarship
~ Community Advisory Board for Campus Apartments–Community Chair

Word Count: 273

Kara M. Fray

Local Address:
604 N. Second
Warrensburg, MO 67568
(660)-793-6758

2 addresses flag a new graduate

Permanent Address:
104 First St.
Columbia, MO 64502
(660)-646-3416

OBJECTIVE

To obtain a position at the Federal Reserve Bank in Kansas City, MO.

EDUCATION

Central Missouri State University
Bachelor of Science in Finance: Financial Services
Financed 100% of education through jobs and scholarships.

Warrensburg, MO   August 2002–Present
Overall GPA: 3.94   Major GPA: 4.0
Begin MBA degree: August 2006

WORK EXPERIENCE

Marketing/Management Department • Office Assistant • Warrensburg, MO   August 2002–Present
- Assist 12 professors and department secretary.
- Perform research for faculty in the department.
- Trusted to enter student grades.
- Responsible for training new assistants.
- Assistant Editor for *Regional Business Review.*

Title in the middle isn't as logical as the title first

Columbia Bank • Teller • Columbia, MO   May 2002–August 2005
- Accurately handle $10,000+ cash daily.
- Provide professional and courteous one-on-one services to clients.
- Responsible for check printing system conversion.
- Accountable for daily functions–printing checks, mailing statements, copying, etc.
- Job offered back for college breaks and summers.

Tri-County Country Club • Assistant Manager • Columbia, MO   Summer 2004
- Collected golf fees and sold various golf products.
- Established and maintained a public relations program for new members, current members, and club events.
- Accountable for managing money and making deposits at bank.
- Job offered back for summers.

ACTIVITIES

Deserves more discussion

- Peer Advisor for Freshman Seminar   Fall 2005
- Alpha Chi Honor Society   October 2004–Present
- Delta Mu Delta Business Honor Society   October 2004–Present
- Marketing/Management Student Interview Team   March 2004–Present
- Order of Omega Greek Honor Society–Greek Week Awards Co-Chair, Vice President   March 2004–Present
- Financial Management Association (FMA)–Treasurer   August 2003–Present
- Students In Free Enterprise (SIFE)–Treasurer, President   August 2003–Present
- Phi Eta Sigma Honor Society   March 2003–Present
- Delta Zeta–Assistant Head Guard, Judiciary Board, Homecoming Co-Chairperson, Historian,   August 2002–Present
        Risk Management, Overall Delta Zeta Homecoming Chairperson, Intramurals,
        Highway Clean-Up, Volunteer at Bristol Manor and Children's Center, Relay for Life,
        Gamma Chi, Class Slate Chairperson

HONORS AND ACHIEVEMENTS

Dates too space consuming

- Delta Mu Delta Top National Scholarship   August 2005–Present
- Financial Executives Institute Scholarship   August 2005–Present
- Sprint Scholarship   August 2005–Present
- Cook-Imes Distinguished Scholar Scholarship   August 2005–Present
- Selected for "Who's Who Among America's College Students"   January 2005
- Nominated for "United States Achievement Academy"   January 2005
- Citizen's Bank and Trust Scholarship   August 2004–Present
- Marshall and Beatrix Ford Scholarship   August 2004–Present
- Selected as 1 of "Top 10 CMSU Sophomores" by Mortar Board   February 2004
- Raymond and Ruth McClurg Scholarship   August 2003–Present
- President's Honor Roll   April 2003–Present
- Delta Zeta "Highest New Member GPA"   March 2003
- Delta Zeta "Highest Big / Lil GPA"   March 2003
- Delta Zeta "Scholar of the Month"   January 2003

Word Count: 512

Kara M. Fray

604 N. Second, Warrensburg, MO 67568 ~ (660) 793-6758 ~ kfray@hotmail.com

OBJECTIVE

To obtain a job at the Federal Reserve Bank in Kansas City, Missouri.

EDUCATION

Central Missouri State University, Warrensburg, Missouri
  Bachelor of Science in Finance: Financial Services–May 2006
  Financed 100% of education through jobs and scholarships

Overall GPA: 3.94 Major GPA: 4.0
Begin MBA degree: August 2006

WORK EXPERIENCE

Office Assistant ~ Marketing/Management Department, Warrensburg, Missouri   August 2002–Present
  Assist 12 professors and department secretary. Assistant Editor for *Regional Business Review.* Perform research for 12 faculty. Trusted to enter students' grades. Responsible for training new assistants. Known as employee always willing to help others.

Peer Advisor for Freshman Seminar ~ Management Department, Warrensburg, Missouri   August 2003–December 2003
  Selected by faculty to help 20 freshmen adjust to college through instruction and academic advisement.

Teller ~ Columbia Bank, Columbia, Missouri   May 2002–August 2005
  Accurately handled $10,000+ cash daily. Provided professional and courteous one-on-one services to clients. Responsible for check printing system conversion. Accountable for daily functions–printing checks, mailing statements, copying, etc. Job offered back for college breaks and summers.

Assistant Manager ~ Tri-County Country Club, Columbia, Missouri   Summer 2004, 2005
  Collected golf fees and sold various golf products. Established and maintained a public relations program for new members, current members, and club events. Accountable for managing money and making deposits at bank. Job offered back for summers.

LEADERSHIP ACTIVITIES

- Students In Free Enterprise (SIFE)–President, Treasurer
- Financial Management Association (FMA)–Treasurer
- Alpha Chi Honor Society
- Order of Omega Greek Honor Society–Greek Week Awards Co-Chair, Vice President, "Being a New Greek"
- Delta Zeta–Assistant Head Guard, Judiciary Board, Homecoming Co-Chairperson, Historian, Risk Management, Overall Delta Zeta Homecoming Chairperson, Intramurals, Highway Clean-Up, Volunteer at Bristol Manor and Children's Center, Relay for Life, Gamma Chi, Class Slate Chairperson
- Delta Mu Delta Business Honor Society
- Phi Eta Sigma Honor Society
- Marketing/Management Student Interview Team

HONORS AND ACHIEVEMENTS

- Delta Mu Delta Top National Scholarship
- Financial Executives Institute Scholarship
- Sprint Scholarship
- Cook-Imes Distinguished Scholar Scholarship
- Delta Zeta "Spark Plug" Award
- Selected for "Who's Who Among America's College Students"
- Nominated for "United States Achievement Academy"
- Citizen's Bank and Trust Scholarship
- Marshall and Beatrix Ford Scholarship
- Selected as 1 of "Top 10 CMSU Sophomores" by Mortar Board
- Raymond and Ruth McClurg Scholarship
- President's and Dean's Honor Roll (all semesters)
- Delta Zeta "Highest New Member GPA," "Scholar of the Month" and "Highest Big / Lil GPA"
- CMSU Honor's Scholarship

"What counts is not the number of hours you put in, but how much you put in the hours." –Unknown

Word Count: 450

■ AGRICULTURE

Jennifer L. Hopper—Ag Business
Jennifer's résumé was the original inspiration behind the makeover edition. Her revised version screams professionalism. Her before version had received a B in another course. Once the résumé is made over, her commendable academic success and ability to juggle work and school is quickly evident to its reviewers.

Adam Thomson—Ag Business
Adam needed to make the transition out of his college wardrobe to a more professional look. After you obtain your first professional position, you need to minimize your education focus and play up your work experience. Adding a profile tied to the employers' needs helps clarify your best attributes.

Keywords for Agriculture

Positions—Sought, Held, or Reported To	Computer Skills	Professional Associations
• Chemical Applicator • Chemical Mixer • Commodities Assistant • Farm Manager • Project Leader • Research Specialist • Ranch Hand • Team Leader	• Microsoft Access • Microsoft Excel • Microsoft Outlook • Microsoft PowerPoint • Microsoft Publisher • Microsoft Word • Quicken • Windows OS • WordPerfect	• Agriculture Club • Farm Bureau Collegiate Chapter • Future Farmers of America (FFA) • National Association MA • National Dairy Association • Rodeo Club

Personality Traits		Degrees, Courses, and Certifications	
• Accountable/dependable • Agriculture driven • Analytical • Aware of current events in agriculture • Budget conscious • Caring • Compassionate • Creative • Dependable • Detail oriented • Easy to get along with • Ethical/honest • Flexible • Hardworking	• Independent worker • Innovative • Multitasker • Organized • Problem solver • Quick learner • Self-motivated • Strong work ethic • Team player • Time-management skills • Troubleshooter • Trustworthy • Works well under pressure	• Bachelor of Science in Ag Business, Plant Science, or Agronomy • Accounting • Ag Econ • Ag Finance • Ag Law • Ag Marketing • Artificial Insemination	• CDL • Farm Management and Record Analysis • Futures Marketing • Hazardous Materials • Sales and Sales Management

Industry Jargon

- Advise farmers
- Aerial and profile graph development
- Agronomy
- Artificial insemination
- Beef
- Biopharmaceutical
- Birthing
- Breeding
- Check brood mares for foals
- Collect, analyze, and evaluate agricultural data
- Conservation programs
- Corn, soybeans, wheat
- Crop management
- Dairy
- Equine
- Equipment maintenance
- Farm financial management
- Feed and water horses
- Genetics
- Gestation periods
- Give medicine to animals
- Groom
- Halter broke yearling filly
- Hazardous materials
- Herbicides
- Infestation
- Laser transit equipment
- Nutrient management
- Order exclusion
- Organize information programs for farmers
- Pesticides
- Plant science
- Poultry
- Swine
- Tack up horses
- Tagging/branding
- Training colts with gentle methods
- Trimble's global positioning satellite system

Jennifer L. Hopper

(Name doesn't stand out)

E-mail jhooper@any.net
404 616th St.
Kersey, CO 89239

1020 University Dr.
313 College Hall
Greeley, CO 80639

(Missing objective or profile)

EDUCATION

Currently attending University of Northern Colorado in Greeley, CO
   Majoring in Agricultural Business and Finance
   Expected graduation date: April of 2006
   Secondary education at Kersey High School,
   Kersey, MO. Graduation year: 2002

(Missing critical GPA and hours worked per week)

WORK EXPERIENCE

Fall 2002–present   **Colorado Valley Bank**   Greeley, CO Teller
Helped customers with transactions in drive through. Balance cash drawer.

Summer 2002   **Heilig Meyers**   Greeley, CO *Sales Associate*
Mike Smith, Manager
Assisted customers in choosing the furniture, appliances,
or electronics that fit their needs. Rearranged and decorated
the sections of our store. Took inventory on every
item in the store. Made sales calls. Used fax machine.

(No numbers quantify job responsibilities)

2000–2001   **Valissa's Flowers**   Kersey, CO *Florist; Sales Clerk*
Mitch Jackson, Owner/Operator
Made arrangements for companies and locals.
Landscaped around local customers' homes.
Assisted customers with ideas on arrangements they can make at home.
Used cash register to complete sales transactions.

SKILLS

(Don't use "I," "me," or "my")

Taken Accounting courses and upper-level math classes:
Statistics, finite math, and economics
Computer Science and Business Computers
Experience with Microsoft Works, Microsoft Word, Excel, Corel, Power point,
and have also used a scanner and designed Web pages.
I have three months' experience in selling retail.

ORGANIZATIONS   Agriculture Club
Sigma Alpha: Professional Agricultural Sorority

(Missing critical honors and activities)

(Too much white space)

Word Count: 232

Jennifer L. Hopper

Dark box allows name to stand out

E-mail jhooper@any.net
Phone (962) 187-0814

1020 University Dr., 313 College Hall
Greeley, CO 80639

OBJECTIVE

Investment Representative for Edward Jones®

EDUCATION

- Bachelor of Science Degree, Double Major: Finance/Agricultural Business   GPA 3.6/4.0   April 2006
- University of Northern Colorado, Greeley
- 100% of educational expenses self-funded through scholarships and working 20 hours per week

WORK EXPERIENCE

Numbers signify responsibility

Colorado Valley Bank   Greeley, Colorado   April 2003–Present
Loan Officer/ Appraiser Internship   Summer 2005
Complete appraisals on real estate and farms ranging from $6,000–$240,000. Obtain records including Deed of Trust, plat, soil type, and aerial maps to assist in valuation. Assist with loan closings and application process. Observe meetings and conference calls to discuss past-due notes and loans in progress. Visit with farmer customers to complete yearly evaluation of property and improvements. Am developing an understanding of the total loan process.

Teller/ Bookkeeper   April 2003–Present
Communicate with customers to complete banking transactions effectively. Trusted to balance and lock vault. Assist customers with safe deposit boxes. Keep updated on computer information, *Telebank* and Internet banking. Take check orders and prepare overdraft lists. Research customer accounts for personal or legal matters. Compile credit reports on customers. Participated in merger with Heritage Bank of Greeley, CO, in February 2005.

Heilig Meyers   Kersey, Colorado   Summer 2002
Sales Associate
Assisted customers in choosing furniture, appliances, or electronics that fit their needs. Rearranged and decorated to increase sales. Took quarterly inventory on every item. Made 20–30 telephone sales calls every morning to prospects and customers. Developed skills in customer relations and gained confidence in closing a sale.

COMPUTER SKILLS

Microsoft Software: Word, Excel, Access, Outlook, PowerPoint, Money
Other: PrintShop Pro, Web page development, Internet Explorer, QuickBooks

HONORS AND ACTIVITIES

Presidential Scholars List (3.5–4.0 GPA)	Sigma Alpha, Professional Agricultural Sorority	Delta Tau Alpha, National Agriculture Honor Society
Ag Ambassadors	~First Vice President	Delta Mu Delta,
American FFA Degree	~Secretary	Honor Society in Business
Agriculture Club	~Scholarship Chair	Administration (top 20% of
~President	~Treasurer	business majors)
~Secretary		

Word Count: 343

Adam Thomson

400 Church Street, Glide, IA 65279
Phone: 912-987-1234 – E-mail: Athomson@hotmail.com

OBJECTIVE

To obtain an Agricultural Insurance Specialist position at Farm Credit Services of Missouri.

EDUCATION

University of Northern Iowa   December 2004
    Bachelor of Science in Agricultural Business

Remove coursework after graduation

Related Coursework:
    Advanced Futures Marketing   Agricultural Marketing
    Agricultural Economics   Farm Management and Record Analysis
    Agricultural Finance   Sales Management
    Agricultural Law   Soil Science

PROFESSIONAL EXPERIENCE

Office Manager   Juergens Produce & Feed Co., Carroll, IA   Jan. 2003–Present
    Maintain and operate multifaceted retail store; formulate feed rations; provide customer
    service to all new and existing customers; manage accounts receivable; maintain food
    drug and fuel inventory; maintain feed mill records.

Veterinary Assistant   Nodaway Veterinary Clinic, Cedar Falls, IA   Nov. 2000–Nov. 2002
    Assisted in many veterinary procedures in the clinic and on location; prepared trucks for
    daily operations with all necessary medicines and supplies; provided customer
    assistance; stocked supplies and prepared displays on the show floor.

Farm Hand   Coffelt Farms, Cedar Falls, IA   Summer 2000
    Successfully maintained feeder cattle operation; performed the basics of farm
    management; assisted with general farm tasks, such as row crop and livestock.

SKILLS

Change to Profile

- Teamwork skills
- Desire to be efficient and productive
- Time management and organizational skills
- Initiative to accomplish goals

ACTIVITIES

- Phi Sigma Kappa Fraternity
- UNI Agricultural Club
- Collegiate Farm Bureau
- United Way volunteer
- Purina Mills Certified Animal Care Advisor
- Iowa Bass Anglers
- Iowa B.A.S.S. Federation
- Iowa Cattleman's Association

Delete college organizations, unless held leadership positions

Word Count: 243

Adam Thomson

400 Church Street ▪ Glide, IA 65279
Phone: 912-987-1234 – Athomson@hotmail.com

OBJECTIVE

To obtain an Agricultural Insurance Specialist position at Farm Credit Services of Missouri.

PROFILE

- Excel in interpersonal communications
- Strong team player who motivates others to achieve teamwork effectiveness
- Demonstrate excellent time-management skills
- Self-motivated individual always looking for ways to improve a process
- Computer skills in Microsoft Office (Word, Excel, PowerPoint, Outlook), Internet Explorer, and Ag Vision

PROFESSIONAL EXPERIENCE

<u>Office Manager</u>   Juergens Produce & Feed Co. ~ Carroll, Iowa   Jan. 2005–Present
- Manage and operate retail store with annual sales of $60,000
- Provide exceptional customer service to customers by establishing relationships and focusing on their needs
- Develop and record radio advertisements, produce live radio broadcasts, write newspaper advertisements, and create attractive flyers for advertising products and services
- Manage accounts receivables by sending bills and receiving payments
- Maintain food drug and fuel inventory and record feed mill inventory
- Organize *Showmanship & Grooming Clinic* and *Horse Owner's Workshop*
- Formulate feed rations

<u>Veterinary Assistant</u>   Nodaway Veterinary Clinic ~ Cedar Falls, Iowa   Nov. 2003–Nov. 2004
- Assisted in veterinary procedures in the clinic and on location, ranging from companion animal vaccination to bovine cesarean sections
- Prepared trucks for daily operations with all necessary medicines and supplies
- Provided customer assistance
- Stocked supplies and prepared displays on the show floor

<u>Farm Hand</u>   Coffelt Farms ~ Cedar Falls, Iowa   Summer 2003
- Successfully maintained 750 head feeder cattle operation
- Performed basics of farm management
- Assisted with general farm tasks, such as row crop and livestock

EDUCATION

University of Northern Iowa ~ Cedar Falls, Iowa   December 2004
    Bachelor of Science in Agricultural Business
    Financed 100% of college education by working 35–45 hours per week
    Involved in Phi Sigma Kappa fraternity, Agricultural Club, and Collegiate Farm Bureau

COMMUNITY ACTIVITIES

Iowa Bass Anglers   Purina Mills Certified Animal Care Advisor
Iowa B.A.S.S. Federation   United Way volunteer
Iowa Cattleman's Association

Word Count: 335

■ COMPUTER SCIENCE AND INFORMATION SYSTEMS

Amy Van de Ven—Management Information Systems
Amy easily obtained an internship in her field with her before résumé. She updated her post-internship version by deleting an unrelated position at a swimming pool and by moving her activities and honors out of their own section and into a subsection under education.

Mary K. Baumli—Office Information Systems
This résumé was showing too much skin (white space). The after version almost doubled in word count and is much more appropriate for the occasion.

Jelani Jones—Office Information Systems
Jelani's before version would have easily qualified for "What Not to Wear" and his after version has been definitely transformed before your very eyes. While both versions contained relevant information, the after version has real selling power. Both skills and accomplishments are woven into his impressive job descriptions.

Keywords for Computer Science and Information System Majors

Positions—Sought, Held, or Reported To	Degrees and Certifications	Personality Traits	Conferences/ Workshops
• Architects	• Bachelor of Science in Computer Science, Management Information Systems	• Accountable	• Cisco
• Assistant		• Analytical	• Novell
• Chief Information Officer		• Creative	• Microsoft
• Chief Technical Officer	• A+ Certification	• Detail oriented	• CES
• Coder	• Cisco Certification	• Ethical/honest	• IEEE
• Computer Lab Assistant	• MCSE	• Independent worker	
• Consultant	• Microsoft Certification	• Organized	
• Designer	• MOUS	• Problem solver	
• Help Desk		• Quick learner	
• Programmer		• Self-motivated	
• Project Leader		• Time-management skills	
• Software Engineer		• Troubleshooter	
• Supplemental Instructor		• Trustworthy	
• Systems Analyst			
• Teaching Assistant			

Industry Jargon and Computer Skills

- Adobe GoLive
- Adobe Photoshop
- Apache
- Audio
- Backend
- Bandwidth
- Bluetooth
- Built personal PC
- C++
- CH
- COBOL
- Cookies
- CorelDraw
- Created Web pages
- Cute FTP
- Database design
- Debug
- Designed Web pages
- DHLP
- Digital cameras
- DOS
- Dreamweaver
- DSL
- E-mail
- Filemaker Pro
- Firewall
- Fireworks
- Flash
- Frontend
- FTP
- GUI
- HTML
- HTTP Server
- IP
- IPX/BPX
- Java
- JavaScript
- LAN
- Linux
- Lotus 1-2-3
- Microsoft Access
- Microsoft Excel
- Microsoft Outlook
- Microsoft PowerPoint
- Microsoft Project
- Microsoft Publisher
- Microsoft Word
- Netscape Communicator
- Netscape Navigator
- Networking
- NIC
- Novell
- NT
- OC
- Oracle
- Ping
- PK zip
- POP Server
- Pop3
- Programming Perl
- Quicken
- Scanners
- SQL
- SQL Plus
- System Analysis
- T1
- TCP/FP
- UML
- Unix
- VB Script
- VB.net
- Visio
- Visual equipment
- Visual Basic
- WAN
- Web Developor
- Windows OS (95/98/ME/2000/XP)
- Wireless
- WordPerfect
- XML
- Association for Computing Machinery (ACM)
- Computer Olympiad
- Digital electronic media club
- AIIP Student Chapter

Amy Van de Ven

Current Address
200 W 19th St.
Maryville, MO 64468
(660) 811-9455

AVandeVen@mail.nwmissouri.edu

Permanent Address
RR 3 Box 47
Grant, MO 65546
(660) 876-1124

OBJECTIVE

To obtain a position as Information Technology or Marketing Intern at Hallmark Corporation for Summer 2004.

PROFILE

- Excellent time-management skills–balance full academic load, 15–25 hours of track practice, and part-time employment while maintaining a high GPA
- Polished presentation and interpersonal skills; dedicated to hard work and willing to take risks
- Exceptional ability to write in a clear, concise, compelling manner
- Computer Skills: Microsoft Word, Excel, PowerPoint, Internet Explorer, Java, COBOL, Adobe Photoshop, Adobe PageMill, typing speed 55 wpm, and Web page maintenance

EDUCATION

Bachelor of Science–Management Information Systems   Overall GPA: 3.78/4.0
Northwest Missouri State University, Maryville, Missouri   **April 2006**
100% of educational expenses funded through academic and athletic scholarships

- Maintained University Honors Scholarship for all semesters
- President's List (1 semester), Dean's List (2 semesters)

PROFESSIONAL EXPERIENCE

University Relations Office ~ Northwest Missouri State University Campus   **Maryville, Missouri**
Editorial Assistant - Northwest Alumni Magazine   **9/02–Present**
Proofread Alumni magazine by checking for errors in spelling, punctuation, and grammar. Collect data from the Internet used for fact checking. Developing attention to detail skills needed for magazine publication. Gaining knowledge of news style article publication techniques.

University Relations Office ~ Northwest Missouri State University Campus   **Maryville, Missouri**
Public Relations Assistant   **9/02–Present**
Writer of articles for *Northwest This Week* newsletter. Time-management skills developed as a result of deadline requirements. Write and submit monthly news releases related to achievements by Northwest students and/or faculty. Contact and correspond with various faculty members. Communicate with students or faculty members that need assistance. Compile data from surveys, and present the information in a report format. Answer phones, take messages, answer questions, send/receive faxes, and make copies.

Grant City Pool   **Grant City, Missouri**
Manager / Lifeguard   **Summer 2001–2002**
Supervised seven employees and three substitute guards. Tracked and deposited daily monetary transactions. Organized Red Cross swimming lessons for 40+ children. Good interpersonal skills developed as a result of many interactions with children and parents. Designated cleaning duties and evaluated employee work. Instructor for private lessons.

ACTIVITIES/HONORS

- ACM - Association for Computing Machinery
- Phi Eta Sigma National Honor Society
- Varsity Women's Track and Field Athlete/Letter Winner
- Volunteer hurdle coach for Junior High and High School students from Bedford, Iowa, Maryville, and Grant, Missouri

Word Count: 404

Amy Van de Ven

Changes made to
add an internship

Current Address
200 West 19th Street
Maryville, MO 64468
(817) 811-9455

AVandeVen@mail.nwmissouri.edu

Permanent Address
RR 3 Box 47
Grant, MO 65546
(660) 876-1124

OBJECTIVE

Obtain a position at Hallmark Corporation.

EDUCATION

Bachelor of Science–Management Information Systems   **Overall GPA: 3.8/4.0**
Northwest Missouri State University, Maryville, Missouri   *December 2005*

- 100% of educational expenses funded through academic and athletic scholarships
- Maintained University Honors Scholarship for all semesters and President's List (2 semesters)
- Dean's List (4 semesters); Phi Eta Sigma National Honor Society; NSCS–National Society for Collegiate Scholars; Delta Mu Delta Business Honor Society
- Varsity Women's Track and Field Athlete/Letter Winner

Computer Skills & Related Coursework:

Systems Analysis & Design	Telecommunications	IT Project Management
Database Systems	Advanced VB.Net	Business Finance
Microsoft Office	Microsoft Project	Macromedia
Dreamweaver	Java	COBOL
Adobe Photoshop	Advanced VB.Net	Microsoft Visio
Unix	Sun Solaris OS	

PROFESSIONAL EXPERIENCE

Northrop Grumman Mission Systems   **Bellevue, Nebraska**
Software Test Engineer Internship   **June 2004–Aug. 2004**

- Tested and developed test steps for JEDI (Joint Enterprise DODIIS Infrastructure) and JMDI (JEDI Multiple Domain Infrastructure) software that is used by the U.S. Department of Defense in military and air force bases all over the country.
- Wrote detailed test steps for the JEDI and JMDI software and was a major team player in developing, editing, and updating the Software and Security Test Document (SSTD).
- Evaluated interfaces between hardware and software and determined operational requirements.
- Performed system administration duties: setting up NIS + environments on Trusted Solaris and Solaris 8 computer systems; tested software that operated on both Unix and Windows operating systems.
- Worked with developers and learned about the software functionality and how to troubleshoot Unix and Windows-related problems. Tested on a variety of Windows systems including Windows 2003 Server, 2000 Server and client, and XP.

Northwest Missouri State University WebTeam   **Maryville, Missouri**
Web Site Maintenance Assistant   **Sept. 2003–Dec. 2004**

- Contributed to the layout, graphic design, linking, networking, and maintenance of www.nwmissouri.edu.
- Proficient with Macromedia Dreamweaver and Adobe Photoshop software.
- Coordinate with University faculty, staff, and department heads to develop and edit content for Web sites.

University Relations and Publications Office–Northwest Missouri State University   **Maryville, Missouri**
Public Relations Assistant   **Sept. 2002–Dec. 2004**

- Wrote, drafted, and proofread articles for *Northwest This Week* newsletter.
- Wrote and submitted monthly news releases to news media publications.
- Worked with Microsoft Access database on a daily basis.
- Answered phones, updated database systems, made copies, faxes, etc.

Alumni Magazine - Northwest Missouri State University   **Maryville, Missouri**
Editorial Assistant Internship   **Sept. 2002–May 2003**

- Proofread and contributed to content and layout of the *Northwest Alumni Magazine*.
- Collected data from Internet publications for background checking, quality control of news releases, flyers, mass e-mails, and brochures.
- Worked on semester-long project that included surveying 3,000 alumni and students to assist editors in marketing decisions for the magazine. Worked directly for Northwest's Marketing Director.

Word Count: 488

206 North Sixteenth
Hopkins, Missouri 64461

Phone 660-888-9990
E-mail mbaumli@hotmail.com

Mary K Baumli

Templates just don't work

Experience

October 1990–Present   Northwest Missouri State University Maryville, MO

Departmental Secretary–Biology / Chemistry / Physics

- ✓ Routine office duties–filing, typing, answering the phone, screening visitors
- ✓ Budget Tracking–two departments
- ✓ Web Design
- ✓ Coordinator of Senior Science Olympiad

November 1989–October 1990   Travis & Bonnett Law Firm   Bedford, IA

Legal Secretary

- ✓ Routine office duties–filing, typing, answering multiline phone system, screening visitors
- ✓ Prepared Guardianship Reports
- ✓ Assisted in tax preparation

Descriptions lack focus on accomplishments

October 1987–November 1987   Ewart Insurance   Bedford, IA

Temporary Secretary

- ✓ Routine office duties–filing, typing, answering phones, screening visitors
- ✓ Evening calling to arrange appointments with clients to discuss insurance options

Education

1992–Present   Northwest Missouri State University Maryville, MO

Two-Year Office Systems Certificate

- ✓ Working toward a two-year office systems certificate. My educational goal is to eventually obtain my BS in Office Systems. I took off a few years to raise my family–I am planning to have my certificate by Fall 2004.

Don't use "I" or "my"

References

Dr. David Smith, Emeritus Biology Faculty
313 US Highway 136
Maryville, MO 64468
660-582-7660
dmshistology@hotmail.com

Dr. Edward L. Farquhar, Emeritus Chemistry Faculty
703 Katy Drive
Maryville, MO 64468
660-582-5024
farq@aol.com

Wasting valuable space with reference information

Ms. Betty Jensen, Executive Secretary to the Dean
336 Keystone Road
Barnard, MO 64423
660-652-3807
jensen@mail.nwmissouri.edu

Word Count: 223

Mary K. Baumli

200 North Sixteenth
Hopkins, MO 64461

Phone 660-888-9990
E-mail: baumli@hotmail.com

OBJECTIVE

Obtain a position as Office Manager with Montereau in Warren Woods.   **Concrete**

PROFESSIONAL EXPERIENCE

October 1990–Present   Northwest Missouri State University   Maryville, Missouri
Departmental Secretary–Biology / Chemistry / Physics

- ✓ Selected by Vice President of Finance to assist in coordination of $15.1 million Garrett-Strong Renovation budget. Tracked all purchase orders for equipment and furnishings for the building. Attended regular meetings to stay on target during renovation with project deadlines.

- ✓ Annually coordinate Senior Science Olympiad. Register 300 participating high school students. Reserve room accommodations for student testing. Organize morning refreshments for instructors and lunch for all students, instructors, faculty, and student support. Order medals and plaques for winners. Compile results for distribution to 100 participating schools.

- ✓ Monitor budget for two departments, reconcile individual accounts with administrative printout. Assist with bid process and purchasing decision to maximize the budget use. Operations accounts totaling $72,000. Monitor individual research accounts ($5,000) and Student Labor budgets ($30,000).

- ✓ Directly supervise two student office assistants. Verify and process 30 student timesheets prior to forwarding to Payroll.

- ✓ Designed Biology departmental Web page–www.nwmissouri.edu/~biology.

- ✓ Presently revamping Chemistry/Physics departmental Web page–www.nwmissouri.edu/~chemphy.

- ✓ Provide quality customer service for 20 faculty members. Maintain confidentiality while abiding by FERPA regulations, screening visitors, typing, and filing.

November 1989–October 1990   Travis & Bonnett Law Firm   Bedford, Iowa
Legal Secretary

- ✓ Prepared guardianship reports. Maintained confidentiality in financial reports; balanced year-end reports.

- ✓ Assisted in tax preparation. Instructed clients in proper way to submit income tax forms.

- ✓ Performed standard office duties–filed, typed, answered multiline phone system, screened visitors.

October 1987–November 1987   Ewart Insurance   Bedford, Iowa
Temporary Part-time Secretary

- ✓ Arranged appointments with clients to discuss variety of life insurance options.

- ✓ Responsible for office duties–filed, typed, answered phones, and screened visitors.

EDUCATION

Two-Year Office Systems Certificate   GPA 3.38   **July 2004**
Northwest Missouri State University   Maryville, Missouri

HONORS & ACTIVITIES

- ✓ Support Staff Council Member–Parliamentarian (2002); Secretary/Treasurer (1996)
- ✓ Support Staff Newsletter Editor / Designer (1998–2000; 2001–Present)
- ✓ Northwest Missouri State University Tower Service Award Recipient (1997)–nominated by peers
- ✓ Phi Delta Kappa Certificate of Recognition for distinguished service to education (1994)

COMPUTER SKILLS

- ✓ Proficient in Word, Excel, PowerPoint
- ✓ Known as a "computer guru" with Office 2000
- ✓ Internet Explorer, Netscape Navigator

- ✓ Dreamweaver 6.0
- ✓ Windows 98 and 2000
- ✓ Outlook, Outlook Express

Word Count: 400

> **Excellent experience goes unrecognized in this bland format.**

Jelani D. Jones
515 W. 7th Street, Apt #4
Auburn, AL 36830 • (334) 541-0915

OBJECTIVE

To obtain a position involving the installation of new computers at the Energizer Battery Plant.

EXPERIENCE

| 11/2002–Present | ADJ Computer Services | Montgomery, AL |

Owner/Operator

*Web site development
*Graphic creation and development
*Data entry
*Document creation (advertising book, flyers, etc.)
*Computer repair and technical support

| 11/2006–Present | Auburn University | Auburn, AL |

Shuttle bus driver

*Drive international students to various locations around Auburn on Saturday afternoons

| 9/2006–Present | Technical School | Auburn, AL |

Computer Instructor

*Instruct adult students in Microsoft Internet Explorer, Word, Excel, Publisher, and FrontPage

| 4/2006–8/2006 | Accent Printing | Auburn, AL |

Graphic Designer

*Designed logos and graphics
*Typesetting
*Waited on customers
*Operated copy machines

| 3/2005–4/2006 | McDonald's | Montgomery, AL |

Cook/Assembly

*Cooked meat
*Assembled sandwiches
*Cleaned kitchen and floors

| 6/2003–8/2005 | Youth Alliance | Montgomery, AL |

Technical Assistant

*Set up and operated computers
*Newsletter design
*Data entry
*Web site updates
*Answered the phone

EDUCATION

| 5/25/2006 | Montgomery Christian School | Montgomery, AL |

Certification

High School Diploma

| In Progress | Auburn University | Auburn, AL |

Certification

Bachelor's Degree in Progress

SKILLS

*Fast and accurate typist (90 wpm)
*Extensive knowledge of all Microsoft Windows operating systems
*Knowledge of reformatting and reloading computer systems
*Broad use of Microsoft Office Suite, Adobe PageMaker, Acrobat, and Photoshop
*Extensive Web design experience
*Ability to deal comfortably with people   **WORD COUNT: 217**

Jelani D. Jones

515 West Seventh Street, Apartment 4 • Auburn, AL 36830
334.541.0915 • jjones@adjcs.com

Objective

To obtain the Administrative Assistant position with Amanda Blu & Co.

Education

Bachelor of Science in Office Information Systems   May 2007
Auburn University, Auburn, Alabama   GPA 3.61/4.00
Juggle three part-time jobs with a combined total of 30–40 hours per week and full-time course load

Computer Skills

Extensive knowledge in all of the following:

• Computer maintenance and repair including both hardware and software
• Microsoft (Windows 95-XP, Access, Word, Excel, PowerPoint, Publisher, FrontPage, Internet Explorer)

• Adobe (Acrobat Professional, PageMaker, Photoshop)
• Jasc (Paint Shop Pro)
• Macromedia (Dreamweaver)
• Intuit (QuickBooks Point of Sale)

Professional Experience

Computer Service Business Owner/Operator
ADJ Computer Services • Montgomery, Alabama   November 2002–Present
Established business during middle school. Use computer skills to solve customer problems such as viruses, ad-ware, upgrade needs. Currently serve over 50 clients and establish new clients by word of mouth. Have developed an excellent ability to listen carefully to customer descriptions of problems.

Computer Teacher
Auburn Technical School • Auburn, Alabama   August 2006–Present
Create and teach lesson plans weekly to classes of adult students. Classes include everything from *First Time Computer Users* to *Advanced Web Design*. The number of students in each class ranges from 4 to 18. Enhanced clear communication and understanding in answering student questions.

Shuttle Bus Driver
Auburn University • Auburn, Alabama   November 2006–Present
Drive 8–10 international students without cars to various locations in Auburn each weekend. Help students locate the various items they need in the Auburn area. Demonstrate patience, understanding the needs of people who do not speak English as their primary language.

Graphic Designer/Customer Service Representative
Accent Printing • Auburn, Alabama   April 2006–August 2006
Designed graphics according to the specifications of customers. Waited on customers. Creativity and originality was demanded for all projects. Learned how to prioritize multiple projects.

Technical Assistant
Youth Alliance • Auburn, Alabama   June 2003–August 2005
Completed computer tasks including Web site design, newsletter creation, computer problem solving, and computer setup as assigned by supervisor. Assisted people outside of the organization with computer questions and setup. Required multitasking and the ability to quickly follow instructions.

Activities and Honors

• Vice President, Auburn Conservatives–Group that promotes conservative values on campus
• Phi Eta Sigma–Outstanding freshman honor society
• Presidential Semi-Finalist Scholarship Recipient–Full Tuition
• Academic Honor Roll, 2 semesters   WORD COUNT: 395

■ CRIMINAL JUSTICE, PSYCHOLOGY, AND SOCIOLOGY

Odessa Hart—Criminal Justice

Odessa's original résumé was overwhelming because of all the dates and overuse of the title Volunteer. Her new version more tastefully displays her unique qualifications in a reader-friendly format.

Naima Maushew—Psychology

Even though she is targeting her résumé to the psychology field, Naima's skills in writing need to really shine through since she also has a degree in English. Her before version may appear acceptable, but the after version is easier to read and makes a powerful first impression.

Lucy Witten—Sociology

Lucy needed to update her wardrobe to focus on her best attributes, her college accomplishments. Her new look helps her educational and professional experiences shine through.

Keywords for Criminal Justice, Psychology, and Sociology

Positions—Sought, Held, or Reported To	Professional Associations	Computer Skills	Degrees and Certifications
• Activities Director • Attorney • Case Manager • Committee Chair • Community services • Crisis Counselor • Group Home Assistant • Judge/Attorney • Legal Secretary • Liaison • Mentor • Paralegal/Lawyer's Assistant • Peer Advisor • Psychology Tech • Researcher • Resident Assistant • Social Worker • Supplemental Instructor • Team Leader • Tutor • Youth Case Worker	• American Bar Association (ABA) • American Psychological Association (APA) • American Sociological Association • Anthropology/Sociology Club • Association for Humanist Sociologists • Criminal Justice Club • National Association of Certified Legal Assistants (CLA) • Psy Chi • Psychology/Sociology Society • Social Psychology Society	• Microsoft Access • Microsoft Excel • Microsoft Outlook • Microsoft PowerPoint • Microsoft Publisher • Microsoft Word • Windows OS • WordPerfect	• Bachelor of Science or Arts in Psychology or Sociology • Bachelor of Criminal Justice • Notary Public • Registered Paralegal (RP)

Personality Traits

• Accountable • Active listener • Adaptive/flexible • Analytical • Caring • Culturally aware • Dependable • Detail oriented • Diplomatic	• Easy to get along with • Empathetic • Ethical/honest • Good listener • Handles confidential information • Leadership abilities	• Patient • People oriented • Positive attitude • Precise • Problem solver • Professional • Quick learner • Resourceful • Responsible	• Sensitive to others • Team player • Troubleshooter • Trustworthy • Unbiased • Understanding • Versatile • Work well under pressure

Industry Jargon			

- ADD
- Addictions treatment
- ADHD
- Adoption
- Advocate
- Affidavits liaison
- Americans with Disabilities Act (ADA)
- Anxiety disorders
- Art therapy
- Behavior management
- Behavioral disorders
- Bipolar personality disorders
- Certified legal assistant
- Child Protective Services
- Children's shelter
- Client files
- Community outreach

- Conflict resolution
- Counseling skills
- Crime victims
- Criminal behavior
- Criminal justice
- Criminal rehabilitation
- Crisis intervention
- Department of Children and Family Services
- Department of Corrections and Probation
- Deposition
- Depression
- Discharge planning
- Divorce agreement
- Domestic abuse
- DSM-IV
- Due process

- Eating disorders
- Elderly services
- Evidence
- Family law
- Family services
- Family therapy sessions
- FBI
- Fingerprints
- Grant writing
- Group therapy sessions
- Individual therapy
- Intelligence testing
- Judicial process
- Juvenile delinquency
- Law enforcement officials
- Legal issues

- Medical professionals
- Motions
- ODD
- Personal injury
- Personality testing
- Pet therapy
- Recreational therapy
- Research analyst
- Social welfare
- Social work
- Subpoenas
- Tax law
- Therapy
- Treatment plan design
- Victim advocate
- Vocational rehab
- Welfare to work
- Wills
- Witness

Odessa Hart

E-mail Address: s318805@mail.nwmissouri.edu
Current Address: 1001 N. Firestone Apt. 7 * Maryville MO 64468 * (660) 582-9777 * (650) 221-9245

OBJECTIVE   To obtain an internship within the human services field working with children, particularly of diverse population and/or victims of any type of abuse

EDUCATION   **Northwest Missouri State University**, Maryville, Missouri
Bachelor of Science–Anticipated Graduation: May 2004
Major: **Sociology** with the Emphasis Option 1: Criminal Justice
Minor: **Psychology**
Major GPA: 3.50   Cumulative GPA: 2.89

Poor format, crowded

RELATED EXPERIENCES

Principal Investigator   Continuous
-Undergraduate research on the process of alienation due to transition from private to public school; research will include interviews, observation, and textual analysis; working towards a publication of our findings; began Fall 2003 and will participate in until graduation

Volunteer   Fall 2003
-Worked with a graduate student at NWMSU; participated in a practicum of individual counseling; able to experience an idea of the character receiving professional help

Volunteer at Children & Family Center of Northwest Missouri   Continuous
-Attended a training course on domestic abuse
-Work Crisis Hotline
-Stay overnight at the shelter when needed open 24/7

Volunteer for Social Problems course   Fall 2002
Northwest Regional Council of Governments, Maryville, Missouri
-Helped Mrs. Brenda Emery, ACCESS 2000 Coordinator, to prepare for workshop presentations for the local youth on entrepreneurship

Volunteer   Fall 2002
-Worked with a graduate student at NWMSU; participated in Body Image Group Therapy sessions she conducted for a class

Volunteer   Summer 2002
-Worked with a graduate student at NWMSU in her study of using animal therapy with children who have autism; decoded videotapes for certain behaviors and/or reactions of the children; name published in thesis on record at Northwest Library

Volunteer for Introduction to Special Education Course   Fall 2001
Adult Basic Education, Maryville, Missouri
-Assisted a South Korean woman to improve her English-speaking and -writing abilities

Observed for Observation and Activity at Elem. School Course   Spring 2001
Horace Mann, Maryville, Missouri
-Observed and worked with children in elementary classroom

WORK EXPERIENCE

Jewelry Sales Associate, Wal-Mart, Maryville, MO   11/03–present
Before-School Aide, Eugene Field Elementary, Maryville, MO   9/03–present
Day Care Employee, Jack & Jill Daycare, Maryville, MO   9/03–present
Janitor, Slagle Janitorial, Maryville, Missouri   10/01–present
Service Representative, K&M Associates L.P., Providence, RI   3/02–present

Dates gone wild

ACTIVITES

K.I.D.S., Secretary   Fall   '00–present
Psych-Soc Society, Public Relations   Fall   '02–present
Acceptance, currently a subsection of Peer Ed   Fall   '02–present
Peer Education, Certified Peer Educator and Advisory Board Member   Spring '03–present
-Emerging Leader Award; attended various conferences

REFERENCES   Available upon request   **Word Count: 408**

Odessa Hart

1001 N. Firestone, Apt. 7 ~ Maryville, MO 64468 ~ (660) 582-9777 ~ s318805@mail.nwmissouri.edu

OBJECTIVE

A position in the criminal justice field working with children, particularly of diverse population and/or victims of any type of abuse.

EDUCATION

> Focuses on relevant learning experiences outside the class

Bachelor of Science   May 2004   Major GPA: 3.5/4.0
Major: Sociology with an emphasis on Criminal Justice; Minor: Psychology
Northwest Missouri State University, Maryville, Missouri
Select Course Highlights
Case Management, Depositions, Evidence Collection & Analysis, Legal Issues & Research

RELATED EXPERIENCES

Research Projects ~ Psychology/Sociology Department ~ Maryville, Missouri
- **Principal Investigator** - Conducting undergraduate research on the process of alienation due to transition from private to public school. Research will include interviews, observation, and textual analysis. Working towards a publication of our findings. (Fall 2003–Present)
- **Research Assistant** - Worked with a graduate student in her study using animal therapy with children who have autism. Decoded videotapes for certain behaviors and/or reactions of the children; name published in thesis on record at Owens Library. (Summer 2002)

Practicum/Observations ~ Northwest Missouri State University ~ Maryville, Missouri
- Assisted graduate student participating in a practicum providing individual counseling to students.
- Cofacilitated in Body Image Group Therapy Session Presentations for 10 classes (Fall 2002)
- Observed and worked with children in 3rd grade at Horace Mann Lab School (Spring 2001)

Volunteer ~ Children & Family Center of Northwest Missouri ~ Maryville, Missouri
- Work Crisis Hotline. Stay overnight at 24-hour shelter when needed. Completed 15-hour training course on domestic abuse. (Fall 2003–Present)

Volunteer ~ Northwest Regional Council of Governments ~ Maryville, Missouri
- Helped ACCESS 2000 Coordinator to prepare for entrepreneurship workshop presented to 100 local youths. (Fall 2003)

Volunteer ~ Adult Basic Education ~ Maryville, Missouri
- Assisted South Korean woman to improve her English-speaking and -writing abilities as requirement in Introduction to special education course. (Fall 2001)

> Use work history section to list less relevant work experience

WORK HISTORY

Jewelry Sales Associate	Wal-Mart ~ Maryville, Missouri	11/03–present
Before-School Aide	Eugene Field Elementary School ~ Maryville, Missouri	9/03–present
Day Care Employee	Jack & Jill Daycare ~ Maryville, Missouri	9/03–present
Service Representative	K&M Associates L.P. ~ Providence, Rhode Island	3/02–9/03
Janitor	Slagle Janitorial ~ Maryville, Missouri	10/01–2/02

CAMPUS ACTIVITES

- K.I.D.S. (Secretary)
- Psych/Soc Society (Public Relations)
- Emerging Leader Award

- Peer Education Certified Peer Educator
- Peer Education Advisory Board Member
- Acceptance Peer Education

WORD COUNT: 391

Naima Maushew

1115 N. College Dr. #106, Salt Lake City, UT 84105
(801) 290-1171
Naimam@hotmail.com

Objective	A position as a human resources manager of a growing company.

Summary of Qualifications

Excellent human resources education, including:
a degree in both English and Psychology, with a minor in General Business; experience with employee personality assessments; technical writing training; tutoring and training experience; organizational mind-set and strong interpersonal communication skills.

Education

- **BS in Psychology**, University of Utah   *2006*
- **BA in English**, University of Utah
- **General Business Minor**, University of Utah
- Will graduate in four years with a 3.5 overall GPA, and was active in five honor societies.

Work Experience

Server, Mandarin Restaurant, Salt Lake City, Utah   *Nov. 2002–May 2006*
- Trained new employees, using an honest and approachable style that resulted in less employee turnover and the manager's confidence in my judgment of each new employee's skills and future at the restaurant.
- Was relied on to supervise employees while the manager was away.
- Was relied on to solve customer problems without consulting the manager.
- Had the skills and knowledge to perform any of the jobs at the restaurant besides cook, resulting in the ability to assist almost any employee with questions or responsibilities.

(Layout wasted space on both sides)

Writing Center Tutor, Salt Lake City, Utah   *Sept. 2004–May 2006*
- Led a laboratory group for developmental English students, resulting in better writers and more passing grades for that course.
- Interacted with several English-as-a-Second-Language students, developing interpersonal, interlingua, intercultural, and interracial skills.

Activities

Editor, *Medium Weight Forks,* student arts annual, Salt Lake City, Utah   *Sept. 2003–May 2006*
- Led an editorial group while choosing works to be included in the annual.
- Developed fund-raising, editing, and publishing skills.

President, Epsilon Gamma chapter, Sigma Tau Delta, English Honor Society, Salt Lake City, Utah   *Sept. 2004–May 2006*
- Organized activities, initiation of new members, and the annual trip to the national conference.

Member, National Honor Societies, University of Utah Chapter
- Alpha Chi   *Oct. 2004–present*
- Phi Eta Sigma   *Nov. 2003–present*
- Psi Chi   *Dec. 2004–present*
- National Society of Collegiate Scholars   *Dec. 2003–present*

References   Available Upon Request

Word Count: 359

NAIMA MAUSHEW

1115 N. College Dr. # 106 ▪ Salt Lake City, UT 84105
(801) 290-1171
Naimam@hotmail.com

PROFILE

Excellent training skills, including a degree in both English and Psychology, with a minor in General Business. Experience with employee personality assessments; technical writing and editing; tutoring and professional presentations.

EDUCATION

Bachelor of Science in Psychology & Bachelor of Arts in English with a business minor   May 2006
University of Utah, Salt Lake City, Utah   Overall GPA 3.85/4.0
- Computer Skills: Microsoft (Word, Excel, PowerPoint, Publisher, Outlook), Internet Explorer
- 50% of educational expenses paid through 3 scholarships and working 25 hours per week

WORK EXPERIENCE

Tutor   Salt Lake City, Utah   August 2004–Present
Writing Center
- Advance the written communication skills of Second Language English and Developmental English students.
- Facilitate long-term learning by coaching positive outlooks and motivating hard work.
- Lead small tutoring groups to support the University's developmental English class curriculum.
- Tutor one-on-one with any university student and concentrate on setting goals and developing and focusing writing.
- Developed communication, teaching, and training skills to better reach students.

Server   Salt Lake City, Utah   November 2002–Present
Mandarin Restaurant
- Knowledgeable on the aspects of each customer service job, including cashier, driver, and server.
- Promote excellent customer service to 50–150 patrons at a Chinese restaurant by paying attention to each table's needs, such as replenishing supplies of food at the buffet and drinks at tables, carrying trays of food to individual tables.
- Train 3–5 employees per year in customer service, food preparation, and cleaning. Fine-tuning the ability to pay attention to detail in a fast-paced environment and the time-management skills to serve up to 25 tables at once.
- Enhancing the aptitude to recognize customers' needs through observation.

LEADERSHIP ACTIVITIES

President   August 2004–Present
Sigma Tau Delta, Epsilon Gamma chapter, English Honor Society
- Organize activities, fund-raisers, selection and initiation of new members, and the annual trip to the national conference. Will present research paper at the 2005 national conference.

Poetry Editor   August 2004–Present
Medium Weight Forks, student arts annual
- Lead an editorial group in selecting poetry to be included in the annual magazine, organize fund-raisers, record minutes at each meeting, support and assist the editor-in-chief, publish 500 magazines per year.

RECOGNITIONS AND HONORS

- Platinum Regents Scholarship
    (3.5/4.0, 6 semesters)
- Phi Eta Sigma, National Freshman Honor Society
- National Society of Collegiate Scholars, Academic Honor Society
- Alpha Chi, National Academic Honor Society

- Psi Chi, National Psychology Academic Honor Society
- Celebration of Quality, Presented research paper

Word Count: 424

5100 W Red Road
Atlanta, GA 68404
Phone (512) 794-4791
E-mail lwitten12@hotmail.com

923 Roberts
Atlanta, GA 68404
Phone (312) 562-9313

Lucy M. Witten

Career Goal:
My career goal is to become a High School Guidance Counselor.

College educational information should be listed first

School Activities and Honors:
High school:
National FFA Organization (9,10,11,12)
———— President (12)
———— Reporter (10,11)
———— Committee Chairperson (10,11,12)
———— Star Green Hand (9)
Future Business Leaders of America
———— Secretary (12)
———— Parliamentarian (10,11)

Fellowship of Christian Athletes (9,10,11,12)
———— Leadership Team Member (10,11,12)
National Honor Society (10,11,12)
Student Council Member (12)
Student Advisory Council Member (10,11)
Band (9,10,11,12)
———— Letter Winner (9,10,11)
Basketball (9,10,11)
———— Letter Winner (11)

College:
Alpha Sigma Alpha Sorority
        Panhellenic Council Delegate
        Assistant Philanthropic Director
        New Membership Committee
        Greek Week Chairwoman
Order of Omega
Students Georgia State Teachers Association

Sigma Pi Sigma Honorary
        Treasurer
Phi Eta Sigma Freshman Honor Society
Agriculture Club

Academic Honors:
High School:
Academic Letter Winner (9,10,11)
Honor Roll (9,10,11)
Outstanding Biology Student Award (10)

Who's Who Among America's High School Students
(9,10,11, 12)
National Honor Society (10,11,12)

College:
President's Honor Roll (2002–2005)
Mortar Board's Top 10 Sophomore Award (2004)
Alpha Chi
Mortar Board

Most high school information should no longer be included

Community Involvement:
High School:
Volunteer Youth Basketball Coach (10,11,12)
Volunteer Community Service Projects:
        Adopt-A-Highway, City Mission volunteer, Sunday school teacher, Vacation Bible School helper, volunteer
        church soloist, Farm Safety instructor, sang carols at nursing home, canned food drive volunteer, school
        greenhouse construction volunteer.
Blue River Community Band Member (10,11)
Kamp 21 After School Day Care Playground/Crafts Volunteer (12)
College:
Beverly Manor Nursing Home Weekly Volunteer (2003–2004)
ASA Adopt-A-Highway
Clothing Drive Volunteer
Kansas City Special Olympics Volunteer
Maryville Children's Center Volunteer

Sections are not in an efficient order

Work experience lacks descriptions

Work Experience:
Researcher–Emory Advisement Assistance (current)
Camp Counselor–Irving Middle Level Day Camp (Summer 2004 and Summer 2005)
Researcher–Emory Psychology Department (August 2003–April 2004, 10 hours weekly)
Salesperson–The Buckle (April 2003–December 2003, 15 hours weekly)
Office Aide–Crete Public Schools (August 2000–August 2003, 40 hours per week)
Receptionist/Internship–Spectrum Psychology Associates (summer 2000, 24 hours a week)
Referee–Crete Parks and Recreation Department (winter 2000 and 2001, 2 hours a week)
Child Care–Various community families (1996–present, hours per week vary)

Word Count: 348

Lucy Witten

923 Roberts
Atlanta, GA 68404

312-562-9313
lwitten12@hotmail.com

OBJECTIVE

High School Career Counselor at an Atlanta public school

EDUCATION

Bachelor of Science, *Emory University,* Atlanta, Georgia
Major in Psychology, Graduation May 2006. Overall GPA 3.90
- Financed through scholarships and working 10 hours per week
- Presidential Scholarship recipient with only 10 awarded each year
- President's Honor Roll for six semesters
- Named Mortar Board's *Top 10 Sophomore* Award recipient
- Committed over 1,000 community service hours in high school

Highlights educational achievements

PROFESSIONAL EXPERIENCE

Emory University – Atlanta, Georgia   Fall 2005 – present
Advisement Assistance Researcher
- Collect student attendance data daily from professors
- Notify Academic Resource Consultants of student absences
  Compile information after gathering results to measure student progress

Irving Middle Level Day Camp – Atlanta, Georgia   Summers 2004 & 2005
Camp Counselor
- Planned daily activities and responsible for 20 middle school age campers
- Supervised and coordinated field trips and service learning outings
- Facilitated activities before and after camp hours
- Developed appreciation for using creativity and flexibility to keep participants actively engaged in activities

Emory University – Atlanta, Georgia   August 2003 – April 2004
Psychology Department Researcher
- Researched child-centered approaches to autism
- Coproduced video for parents introducing them to the child-centered approach
- Selected to present at *Celebration of Quality Symposium*

ORGANIZATIONS & ACTIVITIES

Georgia State Teachers Association – 2004 – present
Alpha Sigma Alpha Sorority – Fall 2003 – present
        Panhellenic Council Delegate, Assistant Philanthropic Director,
        New Membership Committee, Greek Week Chairwoman
Order of Omega – 2003 – present
Sigma Pi Sigma Honor Society – 2002 – present
Phi Eta Sigma Honor Society – 2002 – present
Agriculture Club – 2002 – 2003
Alpha Chi – 2005 – present
Mortar Board – 2005 – present
Phi Alpha Theta Honor Society – 2004 – present

Word Count: 296

KEY ATTRIBUTES:

Hardworking

Focused

Achiever

Creative

Flexible

Leader

ORGANIZED

Responsible

Outgoing

Energetic

Personable

Dedicated

MOTIVATED

Key attributes section jumps out to reader

■ EDUCATION

Marian Janssen—Business Education

Marian's résumé started with the accessories (concrete, accomplishment-oriented descriptions), but some of the wardrobe was outdated. Although the word count barely changed, the new résumé left off high school information so that another college position could be added. The strike-through features were used on the before version to help you see what accessories she needed to shed.

Linda King—Business Education

Using a résumé template instead of creating your own design would be like wearing a uniform to school when it is not required. The personalized format allows for the addition of over 100 words.

Kimberly Thurman—Elementary Education (two-page version)

Two-page résumés are more common in education. Using a professional graphic such as the apple will demonstrate creativity and help this résumé move to the front of the class. Professional references help fill up the second page.

Keywords for Education

Positions—Sought, Held, or Reported To	Degrees and Certifications	Computer Skills	Professional Associations
• Advisor • Coach • Counselor • Intern • Office Assistant • Peer Advisor • Researcher • Resident Assistant • Scholarship Chair • Supplemental Instructor • Teacher • Teaching Assistant (TA) • Team Leader • Tutor	• Bachelor of Science in Elementary, Middle School, or Secondary Education • Certified in the States of _____	• Adobe PageMaker • Boomerang • Centra • Claris Works • Dragon Naturally Speaking • FTP • Hyperstudio • Inspiration • Internet Explorer • Kidspiration • Microsoft Access • Microsoft Excel • Microsoft Outlook • Microsoft PowerPoint • Microsoft Publisher • Microsoft Word • Netscape Composer • Netscape Navigator • Photoshop • Quicken • Windows OS • WordPerfect	• Future Teachers Association • International Reading Association • Junior Achievement Volunteer • Koncerned Individuals Dedicated to Kids (KIDS) • State Teachers Association

Personality Traits

• Accountable • Active listener • Adaptive/flexible • Analytical ability • Caring • Computer literate • Creative • Culturally aware • Customer service skills	• Dependable • Diplomatic • Easy to get along with • Empathetic • Enthusiastic • Ethical/honest • Fast learner • Handle confidential information	• Leadership skills • Motivational • Nurturing • Patient • People oriented • Positive attitude • Problem solver • Professional • Resourceful • Responsible	• Sensitive to others • Strong work ethic • Team oriented • Trustworthy • Unbiased • Understanding • Versatile • Work well under pressure

Industry Jargon

- Accelerated Reader Program
- Assessment tools
- Behavioral management strategies
- Choice Theory discipline
- Class field trips
- Cooperative learning
- Create an environment that enhances student self-esteem
- Curricula
- Designed and implemented lesson plans
- Develop student independent thinking and decision-making skills
- Digitools
- Establish motivational reward systems
- Evaluate students
- Grading rubrics
- Hands-on activities
- Individual learning styles
- Individualized education plans (IEP)
- Interdisciplinary team
- Literacy
- Mainstreamed special needs and gifted students
- Meet needs of visual, kinesthetic, and auditory learners
- Mentor
- Multiple assessment methods
- Observation
- Organized practices and game plans
- Parent-teacher conferences
- PDF files
- Positive reinforcement
- Practicum
- Smart Board
- Special projects
- Speech recognition
- Student motivation
- Tablet PCs
- Telecommunications
- Thematic units
- Wacom pad

Marian Janssen

Local Address
270 Aurora Ave.
Maitland, TN 13911
Mobile: 816.958.3172
Home: 733.172.9694
mjanssen@dell.net

Permanent Address
1694 Ashton St.
Waverly, TX 19376

(Time to lose high school)

• Objective

To obtain employment as a sales and service representative at Bank One Corporation.

(Weak section headings)

• Education

Northwest Missouri State University Maryville, Mo

BACHELOR OF ARTS in Business Education, December 2005

Courses related to Business Education to be completed by Summer 2004

- -Educational Psychology
- -Secondary Teacher Practicum
- -Integrated Software
- -Managerial Communications

~~**DES MOINES AREA COMMUNITY COLLEGE**~~ ~~Ankeny, IA~~

~~**ASSOCIATE OF ARTS**~~   ~~Completion: December 2003~~   *~~Emphasis in Business & Liberal Arts~~*

~~Grade Point Average: 3.91 Cumulative~~   ~~Honors: President's List/Dean's List 4 of 4 semesters~~

(Leave off high school)

~~**MOULTON-UDELL HIGH SCHOOL**~~ ~~Moulton, IA~~

~~**DIPLOMA**~~   ~~Completion: May 2002~~   *~~Emphasis in Business & Mathematics~~*

~~Grade Point Average: 4.11 Cumulative~~   ~~Honors: Class Salutatorian, Honor Roll, Senior Class Vice President~~

• Skills

Software

Windows '98, '00, XP	Microsoft Access (database management)	Microsoft PowerPoint
Microsoft Word	Microsoft Excel	Microsoft Publisher
Global Network (credit card transactions)	Adobe PageMaker	Quicken 2002

• Work Experience

Position: Shift Manager

Creative Innovations   Ankeny, IA   Sep. 2002 – Dec. 2003

- Management of a staff of 15 to 20 Telephone Sales Representatives in a call center environment
  - *After just eight months as a Telephone Sales Representative, I was promoted to Shift Manager due to my consistently high sales figures and high degree of management skills and professionalism*
- Ensuring that sales representatives are meeting and surpassing personal sales goals and quotas
- Human Resources Shift Manager duties, including selection of candidates, interviewing, and hiring
- Training of new employees and monitoring of current staff to ensure that sales goals are being met
- Decision-making responsibilities with regard to terminating those employees that do not meet sales goals
- Hourly sales report generation and figures reporting, database management using **Microsoft Access**
- Comparison of leads to National Do Not Call List registry using **Microsoft Word** & Access

(Italics and bolding distracting)

Position: Production Specialist

Rubbermaid Corporation   Centerville, IA   Feb. 2002 – June 2002

- Operating of plastic molding machine in an assembly-line setting
  - *After only three weeks of employment with Rubbermaid Corp., I received a substantial pay raise & commendation*
- Quality control responsibilities, including separation and recycling/disposal of defective products
- Packing and organization of products to prepare them for distribution to outside vendors

~~• **High School Activities**~~

~~**National Honor Society:** Member. Nationally-recognized organization that recognizes high school students for outstanding scholastic achievement, high moral character, and volunteerism~~

~~**Member of:** Secretary of FFA Chapter, Students Against Drunk Driving, Moulton-Udell Newspaper Staff~~

~~**Sports & Athletics:** Drill Team Captain/Choreographer, Basketball (captain), Volleyball (captain), Softball, Track & Field~~

Word Count: 428

Marian Janssen

Local Address
270 Aurora Ave.
Maitland, TN 13911
Mobile: 816.958.3172

E-mail: mjanssen@dell.net

Permanent Address
1694 Ashton St.
Waverly, TX 19376
Home: 733.172.9694

OBJECTIVE

To obtain employment as sales and service advisor at Bank One Corporation.

EDUCATION

Bachelor of Science Degree with major in Business Education   December 2005
- Northwest Missouri State University, Maryville, Missouri
- Courses related to Business Education to be completed by Summer 2004

Educational Psychology	Integrated Software	Economics I and II
Secondary Teacher Practicum	Managerial Communications	Accounting I and II

- Maintain 30-hour per week employment to assist with college expenses while taking 18 credit hours

Associate of Arts Degree   December 2003
- Des Moines Area Community College, Ankeny, Iowa   GPA 3.91/4.00
- President's List/Dean's List (four of four semesters)
- Worked 30–35 hours a week while attending school full-time

COMPUTER SKILLS

Operating Systems	**Creative Software**	**Financial/Specialized**
Microsoft Windows '98, '00, XP	Microsoft Word	Microsoft Excel
Microsoft Windows NT	Microsoft Publisher	Microsoft Access
Mac OS	Microsoft PowerPoint	Quicken '02

WORK EXPERIENCE

Administrative Assistant

Northwest Missouri State University   Maryville, Missouri   Jan. 2004–Present
- Answer telephone and direct callers/visitors to appropriate departments and professors
- Provide information to students, faculty, and public about services, programs, and schedules at NWMSU
- Make copies of materials and other data for faculty members, file, coordinate incoming and outgoing mail
- Assemble recruiting materials for prospective students
- Relieve faculty of clerical work and minor administrative details

Staff Manager

Creative Innovations   Ankeny, Iowa   Sept. 2002–Dec. 2003
- Managed staff of 15 to 20 Telephone Sales Representatives in a call center environment
- Ensured that each sales representative met or surpassed personal sales goals and quotas
- Selected, interviewed, and hired candidates in high turnover profession
- Trained 100+ new employees and monitored current staff
- Initiated discipline and terminated representatives for not meeting goals
- Prepared hourly sales reports and keyed and managed database using Microsoft Access
- Compared sales leads to National *Do Not Call List* registry using Microsoft Word and Access
- After just eight months as a Telephone Sales Representative was promoted to Shift Manager due to consistently high sales figures and high degree of management ability and professionalism

Production Specialist

Rubbermaid Corporation   Centerville, Iowa   Feb. 2002–June 2002
- Operated plastic molding machine in an assembly-line setting
- Quality control responsibilities included separation and recycling/disposal of defective products
- Packed and organized products to prepare them for distribution to outside vendors
- After only three weeks of employment with Rubbermaid Corp. received a substantial pay raise and recommendation

Word Count: 424

Linda L. King

Summer Contact Information:
801 Chestnut
Winston, FL 59230
Phone: 426-562-8838
E-mail S211666@flsouthern.edu

Campus Contact Information:
512 Roberta Hall
635 University Dr.
Lakeland, FL 58230
Phone 426-874-6549

Resume templates do not work!

Education

August 2003 – May 2007   Florida Southern College   Lakeland, FL

Majoring in Secondary Business Education

3.4 Cumulative GPA

GPA doesn't stand out

~~August 1999 – May 2003   Jackson Co. C-1   Winston, FL~~

~~**High School Degree**~~

~~3.9 GPA~~

~~Emphasis in business courses: Keyboarding, Information Technology, Desktop Publishing, Bus~~
~~Technology I & II, Accounting I, and Economics~~

High school information not needed once in college

Awards received

•Pi Omega Pi Outstanding Underclassman – 2005
•Team Leadership Outstanding Leader – 2005
•Team Leadership Emerging Leader – 2004
•Highest Big Sis/Lil Sis GPA – 2004

Organizations and Leadership Opportunities

•Computer Science Department Peer Advisor – 2004 & 2005
•Florida Girls State City Counselor – 2004 & 2005
•Delta Zeta Sorority – Epsilon Rho Chapter – Pledged 2003
Vice President of Membership – 2005
Greek Week Co-Chair – 2005
Overall Greek Week Committee – 2004 & 2005
Overall Homecoming Committee – 2005
•Pi Omega Pi – Beta Chapter – 2005
Historian – 2005
•National Business Education Association – 2005
•North Central Business Education Association – 2005
Student Representative – 2005
•F-MSTA – 2004

Deserves a description because it is related to target

Leaving off dates allows for attractive two-column format

Work Experience

May 2001 – Present   Mid-West Title Company   Winston, FL

Office Assistant

At Mid-West Title Company, my responsibilities include typing policies, entering data into the computers, filing, answering the telephone, and other miscellaneous office tasks. People skills and office management, in addition to real estate and banking, have both been gained while being employed at Mid-West Title Company.

January 2004 – Present   Curriculum and Instruction Office   Florida Southern — Brown Hall

Student Office Assistant

Don't use "I," "me," or "my"

In the C & I Office, I am responsible for completing various jobs and projects for Elementary Education Professors, including making copies, creating bulletin boards, and typing worksheets. Answering the telephone, distributing the mail, and other miscellaneous office tasks are also performed daily.

Word Count: 270

Linda L. King

Permanent Address
801 Chestnut
Winston, FL 59230
426-562-8838

Local Address
512 Roberta Hall
Lakeland, FL 58230
426-874-6549

E-mail: S211666@flsouthern.edu

Targeted objective

OBJECTIVE

To obtain a secondary business teacher position with leadership and coaching opportunities in the area of girl's volleyball, basketball, and track in the Lee's Summit R-7 School District

EDUCATION

Bachelor of Science in Secondary Business Education   May 2007
Florida Southern College   Lakeland, Florida   3.4/4.0 GPA
- *Work 15 – 20 hours a week while attending school full-time*

COMPUTER SKILLS

- Microsoft Office Suite (Word, Excel, Access, PowerPoint, Photo Editor, Publisher, and Outlook)
- Corel WordPerfect
- Adobe PageMaker
- Dragon Speech Recognition

HONORS

- North Central Business Education Assoc. *Student Representative – 2005*
- Pi Omega Pi *Outstanding Underclassman – 2005*
- Team Leadership *Outstanding Leader – 2005*
- Team Leadership *Emerging Leader – 2004*

WORK EXPERIENCE

CSIS/MIS DEPARTMENT   Lakeland, Florida   August 2004 – Present
Freshman Seminar Peer Advisor
Work closely with Freshman Seminar instructor to provide assistance and advice to incoming freshmen in the Computer Science field. Create activities and group discussions to promote classroom cohesiveness.

Florida Southern–Curriculum and Instruction Office   Lakeland, Florida   January 2004 – Present
Undergraduate Office Assistant
Complete projects for Elementary and Special Education instructors. Type worksheets, file, copy, create bulletin boards, and assist with computer problems. Schedule appointments and direct visitors to instructors' offices. Answer the phone, distribute mail, and communicate professionally with the other offices on the Northwest campus.

Mid-West Title Company   Winston, Florida   May 2001 – Present
Office Assistant
Assist four employees and the office manager with title search and examination. Confer with realtors and lending institution personnel to obtain information regarding customers' files. Use computerized system to retrieve additional documentation needed to complete real estate transaction. Exhibit extreme attention to detail in processing legal documents and descriptions. Prepare and issue policy that guarantees legality of title.

LEADERSHIP OPPORTUNITIES

- National Business Education Association
- Pi Omega Pi – Honor Society for Business Education Majors
   Historian
- Delta Mu Delta – Honor Society for Business Majors
- Tutor Adult with Disability (15 hrs. per week)
- Florida Girls' State City Counselor
- Homecoming Committee
   Awards Committee
- Delta Zeta Sorority
   Vice President of Membership
- Order of Omega – Greek Honor Society
- Greek Week Committee
   Delta Zeta Co-Chair
   Philanthropy Committee

Word Count: 374

Kimberly Thurman

3204 Canyon Road ~ Graham, MO 68117 ~ (817) 922-4300 ~ E-mail: thurman@frontier.com

OBJECTIVE

Enthusiastic, committed, caring educator with a sincere interest in ensuring each child succeeds under my guidance as a fourth grade teacher.

TEACHING EXPERIENCE

Nodaway-Holt Elementary RVII ~ Maitland, Missouri

Fourth Grade Teacher   **July 2005 – Present**

Provide quality instruction to 20+ students of varying ability levels including mainstreamed special needs, gifted/talented, and special education students. Administered Missouri Assessment Program (MAP) state test with 3/14 in Advanced level and 14/21 students in Proficient level. 92% of class is reading on or above grade level.

Valley City Public Schools ~ Valley City, South Dakota

Student Teacher (Grade 3)   **November 2004 – February 2004**

Incorporated technology into creative lessons and created classroom units in Math, Reading, Spelling, and Social Studies for 18 third graders. Gained experience with *Choice Theory* discipline and *Accelerated Reader Program*. Received excellent evaluation from classroom teacher upon completion of 10 weeks.

Student Teacher (Physical Education Grades 9 – 12)   **October 2004 – November 2004**

Designed and implemented lessons that promoted a healthy lifestyle through individual and team activities. Developed and taught *Healthy Heart* unit, including the use of heart rate monitors. Excel at motivating all students to perform at their maximum level.

Practicums   **August 2004 – September 2004**

Physical Education K-12 – Taught use and benefits of heart rate monitors along with aerobic games and skills. *Elementary Education Grade 5* – Worked with a mainstreamed developmentally disabled student. Developed Black History unit. Integrated technology into class assignments.

RELATED WORK EXPERIENCE

Valley City State University (VCSU) ~ Valley City, South Dakota

Viking Ambassador   **August 2002 – May 2004**

Worked with the Office of Enrollment Services to present a positive image of VCSU through campus tours, phone calls, and e-mails to prospective students and parents. Along with other elite, outgoing students, planned activities for student body such as care packages over holidays and helped with moving in.

Student Center Administrative Assistant   **September 2002 – May 2004**

Served as secretary performing a variety of administrative functions including setting up meetings and business gatherings.

Learning to Live Instructor   **August 2002 – May 2003**

Provided learning instruction to a group of 15 freshman students. Acquainted students with the University's technology systems, helped with adjustments students make, and presented skills they needed to succeed in higher education through community service projects and ropes courses.

Resident Assistant   **August 2002 – May 2003**

Promoted family atmosphere for 100+ students while maintaining safety of all residents. Coordinated activities and programs to help students excel at school while offering advice in time management and self-confidence.

North Central School System ~ North Central, South Dakota

Volleyball Coach   **November 2002 – 2003**

Served as head Junior High Girls and Assistant Varsity Women's volleyball coach. Implemented practice and game plans for a 15-girl roster.

Tower City School System ~ Tower City, South Dakota

Softball Coach   **May 2001 – August 2001**

Organized practices and drills and coached games for 13 and under girls. Developed player skills while promoting good sportsmanship.

Kimberly Thurman – Page 2

EDUCATION

Bachelor of Science in Education   **May 2005**
Double Major: Elementary Education (1st – 6th) and Physical Education (K – 12th)
Valley City State University ~ Valley City, South Dakota   GPA 3.85/4.0
Self-financed 100% of education with academic and athletic scholarships while working 15 hours per week.

Accomplishments
Department of Health and Physical Education – Top Senior Academic Award
Who's Who of American Students   President and Dean's List
Varsity Volleyball and Softball   Academic All American

TECHNOLOGY SKILLS

MS Word   Photoshop   Internet Explorer
MS PowerPoint   Inspiration   Netscape Navigator
MS Access   Kidspiration   Netscape Composer
MS Excel   Hyperstudio
Claris Works   GroupWise Email

PROFESSIONAL REFERENCES

Ms. Karma Smith   Ms. Sydney Snow
Principal   Curriculum and Instruction Faculty/Advisor
Nodaway-Holt Elementary R-II   Valley City State University
318 South Taylor   300 College Way
Maitland, MO 68117   Valley City, SD 58072
Ksmith@k-12missouri.edu   Ssnow@mail.valleystate.edu
660-939-2135   701-845-5555

Ms. Lisa Loe   Mr. Ridge Yount
Principal   Curriculum and Instruction Faculty
Valley City Public Schools   Valley City State University
200 First Street   300 College Way
Valley City, SD 58072   Valley City, SD 58072
Lloe@k.12southdakota.edu   Ryount@mail.valleystate.edu
701-845-1234   470-333-1324

PROFESSIONAL PORTFOLIO AVAILABLE

Word Count: 680

■ HEALTH CARE

Jaque Anderson—Athletic Trainer (Two-Page Version)

Jaque's experience was phenomenal, but the presentation of her qualifications lacked finesse. Better utilization of white space and jazzing up her section headings really enhanced the résumé. She still needs a two-page format but was able to add both a professional profile and her references to the revamped version.

Chao-Ju Hang—Medical Assistant

Sometimes outerwear (such as a professional trench coat or a page border) can enhance the overall impression of an applicant or his or her résumé.

Ashley Weybrew—Nurse

Ashley shows that a little makeup can go a long way. Many applicants in a professional field will use a template to display their skills, but designing her own résumé and adding a creative element such as clip art will set her apart from her peers.

Abby Hanks—Occupational Therapist

Abby came up with innovative ways to stretch her word count by adding courses and expanding on her leadership experience. Course names may come up as hits for keywords in some résumé tracking programs.

Michael Spencer—Office Manager

Michael's before version reminded me of an outdated leisure suit; he's definitely stepping out in style with his revised format. Eliminating the "I's" enhances the focus of his résumé.

Davis Platt—Personal Trainer (Two-Page Version)

Davis needed a two-page version to showcase all his muscles (accomplishments). Using clip art in his section headings helps showcase his skills and ensures that his résumé makes it to the top of the heap.

Anna Paige Hughes—Pharmacist

Anna needed to reformat her résumé to enhance its readability. The polished after format shows she can conquer clutter and highlight her skills in a fresh, crisp manner.

Keywords for Health Care Careers

Positions—Sought, Held, or Reported To		Personality Traits	
• Athletic Trainer	• Medical Specialist	• Accountable	• Negotiation skills
• Case Manager	• Mentor	• Active listener	• Patient
• Circulating Nurse	• Occupational	• Adaptive/flexible	• People oriented
• Clinical Supervisor	Therapist	• Analytical	• Precise
• CNA	• Patient Care Assistant	• Caring	• Problem solver
• Committee Chair	• Peer Advisor	• Dedicated	• Professional
• Crisis Counselor	• Pharmacy Intern	• Dependable	• Quick learner
• Emergency Medical	• Pharmacy Tech	• Desire to help others	• Resourceful
Technician (EMT)	• Research Associate	• Detail oriented	• Responsible
• Dental Hygienist	• Researcher	• Diplomatic	• Sensitive to others
• ER Staff Nurse	• Resident Assistant	• Easy to get along with	• Sympathetic
• Group Home Assistant	• Staff LPN	• Empathetic	• Team player
• HMO Case Manager	• Staff Nurse	• Ethical/honest	• Troubleshooter
• Lab Assistant	• Staff Pharmacist	• Handles confidential	• Trustworthy
• Labor and Delivery	• Supplemental	information	• Understanding
Charge Nurse	Instructor		• Versatile
• Medical Assistant	• Team Leader		• Work well under pressure

Degrees and Certifications		Computer Skills	Professional Associations
• AED • Advanced Cardiac Life Support Certification • Associates Degree in Applied Science of Nursing • Bachelor of Science in Applied Nursing • Certified Medical Assistant • Certified Pharmacy Technician (CPhT) • Diploma in Licensed Practical Nursing • Doctor of Pharmacy Degree	• Emergency Nursing Pediatric Certification • EMT Certification • External Fetal Monitor Certification • Master of Science Degree in Athletic Training • National Licensing Exam • State Internship License • State License	• Advance PCS • Caremark • Database entry • Discount Cards • Express Scripts • Microsoft Access • Microsoft Excel • Microsoft Outlook • Microsoft PowerPoint • Microsoft Word • Windows OS • WordPefect	• American Council on Exercise (ACE-PT) • National Association of Pharmacy & Therapeutic Committee • American Association of Medical Assistants • NATABOC • National Athletic Trainers' Association • Fellowship of Christian Athletes

Industry Jargon			
• Administer EKGs and X-rays • Administer medications • Advocate • American with Disabilities Act (ADA) • American Sign Language (ASL) • Assess, plan, and monitor drug programs • Assist in convalescence and rehabilitation • Assist physicians • Buy medical supplies • Community outreach • Complete third-party insurance forms • Conflict resolution • Counseling skills	• Corporate wellness • Develop new drugs • Develop treatment plans • Discharge planning • Dispense medications • Domestic abuse • Draw blood • Dress wounds and incisions • Educate patients • Ensure records are maintained • Give advice about diets and exercise • Grant writing • Help patients cope with illness • HIPPA training • Keep confidential records • LPN	• Make sterile solution • Manage nursing care plans • Maintain medical records • Medical professionals • Medical terminology • Monitor health and progress of patients • Monitor vital signs • Order supplies and equipment • Patient counseling • Perform invasive procedures • Prepare infusions	• Prepare examination rooms • Prevent disease and injury • Promote health • Provide bedside nursing care • Provide information about medications • Rehabilitation • Research for pharmaceutical manufacturers • SOAP note documentation • Take vital signs • Treatment plan design • Troubleshoot insurance claims

Jaque Anderson, MS, ATC, LAT

700 Highland Avenue ▪ **Maryville, MO 64468** ▪ **660.582.1311** ▪ **Janderson@hotmail.com**

Two-page résumés are often appropriate

PROFILE

Results-oriented certified Athletic Trainer with a track record of providing exceptional injury prevention, recognition, treatment, and rehabilitation to athletes at the collegiate and high school level. Eager to stay at the top of the profession by learning new and innovative techniques. Excel at communicating with athletes and coaches to ensure needs of both teams and individual athletes are being met.

EDUCATION & CERTIFICATIONS

Master of Science in Athletic Training
West Virginia University, Morgantown, West Virginia

May 2003
GPA 3.88/4.0

Bachelor of Science, Double Major in Biology & Psychology
Northwest Missouri State University, Maryville, Missouri

December 2000
GPA 3.49/4.0

AED Instructor certified by NATABOC, June 2004
American Red Cross CPR & First Aid, 1995 – current
AED certified by NATABOC, May 2002 – current

Approved Clinical Instructor, August 2002
Examiner Training Program, June 2001
Certification Number – 010102010

PROFESSIONAL EXPERIENCE

Athletic Trainer ▪ Northwest Missouri State University, Maryville, Missouri ▪ Aug. 2003 – current
- Provide coverage for football and women's basketball at a D-II University. Formulate and monitor rehabilitation for 400 male and female athletes. Teach *Care and Prevention of Athletic Injuries* to 20–30 college students each semester. Supervise four Graduate Assistant Athletic Trainers and mentor their development. Formulate the athletic training inventory and annual budget of $17,000. Maintain SOAP note documentation. Refer to Physicians and coordinate aftercare as needed.

Graduate Assistant Positions ▪ West Virginia University, Morgantown, West Virginia ▪ Aug. 2001 – May 2003

Head Athletic Trainer University High School
- Provided coverage for 17 AAA High School Sports covering male and female athletes. Initiated prevention, evaluation, and rehabilitation of athletic injuries. Administered on-field emergency care. Maintained SOAP Note Documentation. Coordinated daily treatments. Created yearly athletic training inventory and budget of $5,000. Traveled with football and sports teams that went to district and state events. Supervised four undergraduate and graduate Athletic Trainers from WVU. Communicated with athletes, parents, coaches, outside medical providers, and administration to ensure highest quality care was provided.

Clinical Athletic Trainer at HealthWorks Rehab and Fitness
- Provided Clinical Outreach coverage for swimming, soccer, and basketball two mornings each week. Assisted in rehabilitation of patients by helping them relieve pain, increase mobility, and reestablish use. Obtained exposure to Aquatic Therapy.

Athletic Training Intern ▪ Disney's Wide World of Sports Lake Buena Vista, Florida ▪ Jan. – May 2001
- Provided coverage for visiting athletes participating in softball, lacrosse, track and field, cheerleading, baseball, basketball, volleyball, dance, field hockey, and gymnastics. Administered on-field emergency care of athletic injuries. Observed orthopedic surgeries.

Jaque Anderson, MS, ATC, LAT – Page 2

<u>**Athletic Training Student**</u> • Northwest Missouri State University, Maryville, Missouri • Aug. 1996 – Dec. 2000
- Exposed to athletic training at high school and collegiate level. Worked with Division II varsity football (twice during 15-game season resulting in NCAA D-II National Championships, once during MIAA conference championship season), NCA cheerleading and boy's basketball camps, varsity women's soccer, men's and women's outdoor and indoor track and field and Maryville High School football and basketball program.

<u>**Nurse Technician & Unit Clerk**</u> • St. Luke's Northland Hospital , Kansas City, Missouri • May 2000 – Aug. 2000
- Assisted in patient care (wound care, minor surgical procedures) in Emergency Room. Monitored vital signs. Transported Patients to ICU, PCU, and OR. Stocked room and surgical supplies. Ordered lab work and X-rays.

PROFESSIONAL ACTIVITIES & HONORS

Careers in Athletic Training, Presenter at King City R-1 School District, April 2005
NATABOC Examiner/Model, Jan. 2005, June 2004, Nov. 2003
Mid-Atlantic Athletic Trainers' Association, 2001 – 2003
National Athletic Trainers' Association, 1996 – current
NATA Clinical Meeting and Symposium – 2004, 2001, 2000, 1999, 1998
Mid-America Athletic Trainers' Association, 1996 – current
MAATA District Meeting – 2005, 2000, 1999, 1998
Missouri Athletic Trainers' Association, 1996 – current
MOATA State Meeting – 2004, 2000, 1998
Northwest Student Athletic Trainers' Association, 1996 – 2000
   *Treasurer 1999 – 2000
   *President 1998 – 1999
Cocoordinator of Coaches Sports Medicine Clinic, 1999

Layout and Design of the Athletic Training Room, MAATA District Student Presenter, 1998
Fellowship of Christian Athletes, 1996–2000
Camp Quality Companion, 1997, 1999
National Athletic Trainers' Association Graduate Scholarship, 2002
National Athletic Trainers' Association Undergraduate Scholarship, 2000
Northwest Missouri State University Outstanding Leadership Award, 2000
Mid-America Athletic Trainers' Association Undergraduate Scholarship, 1999
Mortar Board Turret Chapter Member, 1999 – 2000
   *Treasurer 1999 – 2000
Cardinal Key National Honor Sorority, 1998 – 2000
   *Historian 1998 – 1999
Blue Key National Honor Fraternity, 1998 – 2000
   *President 2000 – 2001
Alpha Chi National Honor Society, 1998 – 2000
Northwest Missouri State University Regents Scholarship, 1996 – 2000

REFERENCES

Laura Thomson, MS in Ed., ATC/R
Head Athletic Trainer
Athletic Department
Northwest Missouri State University
800 University Drive
Maryville, MO 64468
(660) 562-1300
Lthomson@mail.nwmissouri.edu

Jordan Reichert, MS, ATC
Director, Athletic Training Services
HealthWorks Rehab and Fitness
943 Maple Drive
Morgantown, WV 26505
(304) 285-3821
Jreichert@aol.com

Susan Bostwick, PhD, ATC
Graduate Athletic Training Program
School of Physical Education
West Virginia University
P.O. Box 6116
Morgantown, WV 26505-6116
(314) 293-3200 x5225
SBostwick@mail.wvu.edu

Brittany Farlow, PT, ATC
President
HealthWorks Rehab and Fitness
943 Maple Drive
Morgantown, WV 26505
(304) 599-2515
Bfarlow@healthworksrf.org

Word Count: 849

Chao-Ju Chang

Current Address: 316 Song Hall, Corvallis, OR 93112 (293) 844-3672
Permanent Address: 8077 W. 61st Plaza, Albany, OR 63711   (618) 657-2775
E-Mail Address: Cchang@mail.osu.edu

Add courses related to the internship

OBJECTIVE
To secure a medical assistant position.

EDUCATION
Associate Degree   May 2008
Oregon State University, Corvallis, Oregon

RELATED EXPERIENCE
INROADS Intern
Liberty Mutual-group disability claims unit, Albany, OR   Summer 2004 & 2005

Expand on manager type activities

- Received and entered illness recovery claims into system daily. Screened claims for any red flags. Contacted claimant and employer to collect information needed to complete claim and triage to appropriate case manager.
- Assisted about 50 claimants per day with questions regarding claim over the phone. Entered notes and updated information into system.
- Completed the MAGIC® course in which customer service skills were critiqued

Shift Manager
Subway, Albany, OR   July 2001–August 2002

- Received keys to the store and safe
- Opened and closed store
- Responsible for the amount of cash accessible in store during shift
- Counted inventory

WORK EXPERIENCE
Sales Associate/Cashier, Finish Line, Albany, OR   July 2003–August 2004
Sales Associate, Footlocker, Albany, OR   August 2002–May 2003
Volunteer, Adult Education and Literacy, Corvallis, OR   February 2005–April 2005

COMPUTER SKILLS
Internet Explorer, Microsoft Word, PowerPoint, Excel, Microsoft Outlook

ACTIVITIES/ORGANIZATIONS
- Ad Ink (advertising club)–Campaigns committee
- American Marketing Association
- Mentors Over Retention and Education–Mentor

Word Count: 231

Chao-Ju Chang

Current Address: 316 Song Hall, Corvallis, OR 93112 (293) 844-3672
Permanent Address: 8077 W. 61st Plaza, Albany, OR 63711 (618) 657-2775
Cchang@mail.osu.edu

OBJECTIVE

A position as a Medical Assistant providing routine clerical and clinical duties to enhance the efficiency of Dr. Pat Dawson's practice. Possess excellent organizational and communication skills that will be used to ensure patients are well cared for.

EDUCATION

Associates Degree ~ Oregon State University, Corvallis, Oregon   May 2008

Pursuing Certificate as a *Certified Medical Assistant* to be completed May 2008
Relevant Coursework

- Anatomy & Physiology
- Medical Terminology
- Typing and Transcription

- Accounting I & II
- Using Computers
- Record Keeping

Computer Skills: Internet Explorer, Microsoft (Word, PowerPoint, Excel, Outlook)

RELATED EXPERIENCE

INROADS Intern
Liberty Mutual-Group Disability Claims Unit ~ Albany, Oregon   *Summer 2004 & 2005*
- Received and entered illness recovery claims into system daily. Screened claims for any red flags.
- Contacted claimant and employer to collect information needed to complete claim and triage to appropriate case manager.
- Assisted approximately 50 claimants per day with questions regarding claim over the phone.
- Entered notes and updated information into system.
- Successfully completed the MAGIC® course in which customer service skills were critiqued.
- Consistently received excellent end-of-the-summer evaluations.

Shift Manager
Subway ~ Albany, Oregon   *July 2001–August 2002*
- Supervised and delegated work for up to three employees. Aided in the training of new hires.
- Trusted with keys to the store and safe. Opened and closed store. Responsible for counting accessible cash in store as well as bread upon the opening and/or closing of the store.
- Assisted store manager with counting inventory.

WORK HISTORY

INROADS Intern ~ Liberty Mutual, Albany, Oregon   Summer 2004 & 2005
Sales Associate/Cashier ~ Finish Line, Albany, Oregon   July 2003–August 2004
Sales Associate ~ Footlocker, Albany, Oregon   August 2002–May 2003
Shift Manager ~ Subway, Albany, Oregon   July 2001–August 2002

ACTIVITIES / ORGANIZATIONS

- Ad Ink (advertising club)
- Biology Club

- Mentors Over Retention and Education ~ Mentor

Word Count: 338

1000 West First Street   Phone 660-562-3100
Maryville, MO 64468   E-mail Aweybrew@classicnet.net

Ashley Weybrew

(Templates just don't work)

Experience   October 1994 – Present   St. Francis Hospital   Maryville, MO

House Supervisor (2/2003 – Present)
- ✓ Charge nurse over several units
- ✓ Provide care in ER, OB, med-surg, mental health, and surgery

Labor & Delivery Charge Nurse (6/2000 – 9/2004)
- ✓ Monitor patients in labor and delivery

Circulating Nurse & ER Charge Nurse (2/2001 – 2/2003)
- ✓ Get patients ready for surgery and provide intraoperative care
- ✓ Triage and care for all ages of patients in ER

Staff LPN in Labor & Delivery (7/1994 – 6/2000)
- ✓ Assisted with labor patients and newborns

May 1995 – June 1998   Family Medicine Associates   St. Joseph, MO

Office Nurse
- ✓ Routine duties – answered multiline phone system and managed call-ins, prepped patients for physicians
- ✓ Set up referrals
- ✓ Assisted in helping low-income patients

(Descriptions lack focus on accomplishments)

August 1994 – May 1995   Northwest OB/GYN   Maryville, MO

Office Nurse
- ✓ Routine duties – answered multiline phone system and got patients ready for their visit
- ✓ Evening calling to arrange appointments with clients to discuss insurance options

Education   **UMKC School of Nursing**
- ✓ Working toward a MSN. My educational goal is to eventually obtain my Medical Practitioner Degree. I already have my AA Degree and LPN.

(Don't use "I" or "my")

References   Dr. Jeremy Troshynski, UMKC Faculty Advisor
313 US Highway 136
Kansas City, MO 68466
816-453-7660
Jtroshynski@hotmail.com

Dr. Melissa Bewley, St. Francis Hospital
200 South Hills Drive
Maryville, MO 64468
660-582-2600
APHughes@stfrancis.net

Dr. Eric Shelley, OBGYN
200 South Hills Drive
Maryville, MO 64468
660-582-2525
Esheley@familymedmail.net

(Wasting valuable space with reference information)

Word Count: 250

Ashley Weybrew

1000 West First Street
Maryville, MO 64468

660-562-3100
aweybrew@classicnet.net

OBJECTIVE

Family Health Nurse Practitioner

PROFESSIONAL EXPERIENCE

St. Francis Hospital ~ Maryville, Missouri   **1994 – Present**
House Supervisor (2/2003 – Present)
Function as charge nurse over 5 different units. Delegate assignments and serve as
resource person. Provide exceptional patient care to patients in each area (ER, OB,
med-surg, mental health, and surgery). Known as knowledgeable and caring nurse
committed to the needs of patients and their families.

Labor and delivery charge nurse (6/2000 – 9/2004)
Monitored labor and delivery patients, provided postpartum care, assisted in C-sections,
provided care to newborns in level 3 nursery; NALS and external fetal monitor certified.

Circulating nurse, orthopedic surgery (2/2001 – 2/2003)
Prepared patients for surgery; assisted anesthesiology, physician, and scrub techs as
needed, provided intraoperative care.

ER charge nurse (7/2001 – 2/2003)
Triaged and cared for patients from newborn to geriatric age, stabilized emergency
patients, assisted physician. ENPC certified.

Staff LPN-labor and delivery (7/1994 – 6/2000)
Assisted in the management of labor patients, newborn and postpartum care.

Family Medicine Associates ~ St. Joseph, Missouri   **May 1995 – June 1998**
Office Nurse, Family Practice
Primarily assisted one family physician but could assist any of 9 partners in family
practice setting. Managed phone call-in messages from patients, readied patients
for visit with doctor, set up referrals, assisted low-income patients to obtain needed
medications by working with drug companies, assisted physicians with procedures.

Northwest OB/Gyn ~ Maryville, Missouri   **Aug. 1994 – May 1995**
Office Nurse, Obstetrical and Gynecological
Assisted physicians with gynecological procedures, readied patients for physician visit.
Managed patient phone calls, set up referrals, took histories of new OB patients and
educated patients on prenatal care.

EDUCATION

University of Missouri-Kansas City School of Nursing, Kansas City, Missouri
Senior in Bachelor's of Nursing program currently, enrolled in RN to MSN

Southwestern Community College, Creston, Iowa
Associates Degree in Applied Science of Nursing, 5/1999 – 6/2000

Northwest Missouri State University, Maryville, Missouri
Nursing prerequisites and general education courses, 1/1998 – 5/2004

Northwest Technical School, Maryville, Missouri
Diploma in Licensed Practical Nursing, 8/1993 – 8/1994

TRAINING
♦   Advanced Cardiac Life Support Recertification, October 2004
♦   External Fetal Monitor Certification, August 2003
♦   Emergency Nursing Pediatric Certification, May 2003

VOLUNTEER
♦   Business Professional Women's Organization
♦   SEA shared governance council, St. Francis Hospital, chairperson for 3 years

---

Attributes

Patient

Focused

Caring

Resourceful

Dedicated

Team oriented

Organized

Honors

2000 HOSA
Bowl 3rd
Place
National
Winner

2000 HOSA
Bowl 1st
Place
3rd Place Medical
Terminology
Iowa State
Winner

**Word Count:
355**

Abby Hanks

285 North Wing	601-933-7415	
150 Memorial Drive	Ahanks@hotmail.com	505 NW Hampton
Lawrence, KS 75744		Kansas City, MO 65899

Education

Bachelor of Science in Occupational Therapy   **May 2006**
University of Kansas, Lawrence, Kansas
- GPA - 3.07/4.0

College Preparatory Diploma   **May 2002**
Lincoln College Preparatory Academy   Kansas City, MO
- GPA - 3.4/4.0

Experience

Member Service Representative (Intern)   **May 2003-Present**
Mazuma Credit Union   Kansas City, MO

This format doesn't work for those with lots of information

- Balanced, opened, and closed drawer daily with amounts of up to $65,000.
- Enforced the law on holding checks, for how long and reasons why (Regulation CC).
- Provided great customer service to up to 185 members per day.
- Resolved, listened to, and corrected problems with unsatisfied members.

Volunteer Experience

Group Leader   **June 2002**
Conquering Life's Challenges Academy   Kansas City, MO
- Responsible for supervising 10 children.
- Acted as a liaison between parents, children, and staff.
- Helped with meal preparation and enrichment activities.

Admissions Volunteer   **January 1999**
North Kansas City Hospital   Kansas City, MO
- Escorted patients to their hospital rooms.
- Responsible for sending and receiving confidential records through the hospital mail system.
- Ran any other errands assigned to me to help the department run smoothly.

Computer Skills

Proficient in Microsoft Word, Microsoft Excel, Microsoft Outlook, Microsoft PowerPoint, e-mail.

Save room by putting computer skills with education

Activities

Delta Sigma Theta Sorority, Inc. Nu Gamma Chapter
Vice President and Charter Member
- Performed countless public service events.
- Sponsored forums and other enrichment events in the areas of: physical and mental health, educational development, economic development, international awareness and involvement, and political awareness and involvement.

Mentors Over Retention Education (M.O.R.E)
- Helped a first-year freshman with the transition of going to college.
- Guided students in setting and attaining goals.

Word Count: 287

Abby Hanks

285 North Wing
150 Memorial Drive
Lawrence, KS 75744

601-933-7415
Ahanks@hotmail.com

505 NW Hampton
Kansas City, MO 65899

OBJECTIVE

To obtain field experience in occupational therapy at a first-class hospital over summer break 2005.

EDUCATION

Bachelor of Science Degree, Occupational Therapy   **May 2006**
University of Kansas, Lawrence, Kansas   GPA - 3.07/4.0
Will pursue Master's degree in Occupational Therapy
Member of AOTA (American Occupational Therapist Association)

Relevant coursework to be completed by Summer 2005
Biology (9 hours), Human Anatomy & Physiology (6 hours), Psychology (12 hours), Employment Staffing and Selection Principles (6 hours), Orientation to Occupational Therapy (6 hours), Medical Terminology & Ethics (9 hours)

College Preparatory Diploma   **May 2002**
 Lincoln College Preparatory Academy ~ Kansas City, Missouri   GPA - 3.4/4.0

Computer Skills - Proficient in Microsoft Office (Word, Excel, Outlook, PowerPoint), e-mail, and Internet searches

WORK EXPERIENCE

Member Service Representative   **May 2003 – Present**
Mazuma Credit Union ~ Kansas City, Missouri
      Balanced, opened, and closed cash drawer daily with amounts of up to $10,000. Enforced Regulation CC (the Federal regulation determining how long to hold checks). Provided exceptional customer service to 150 – 185 members per day. Listened to and resolved member concerns. Maintained confidential information.

LEADERSHIP EXPERIENCE

Vice President and Charter Member   **March 2003 – Present**
Delta Sigma Theta Sorority, Inc. Nu Gamma Chapter
   ▪ Founding member of organization.
   ▪ Coordinate and participate in over 10 public service events per semester, such as painting the home of an elderly area couple, sorting clothes at the Family Crisis Center, performing as a Team Leader on Martin Luther King Day of Service, distributing self-examination charts for Breast Cancer Awareness Month, assisting freshmen during "Exploring Majors." Sponsor a weekly group "Sister Circle" to discuss relevant issues regarding women on campus.
   ▪ Sponsor forums and other enrichment events in the areas of physical and mental health, educational development, economic development, international awareness and involvement, and political awareness and involvement.

Mentors Over Retention Education (M.O.R.E)   **September 2003 – Present**
   ▪ Successfully helping an "at-risk" freshman with the transition of going to college and in setting and attaining goals. Recommend campus resources and monitor student's performance while at school.

Governor's Student Leadership Forum   **January 2004**
   ▪ Nominated to attend statewide forum by Student Senate.
   ▪ Attended leadership seminars led by successful leaders.
   ▪ Met with Missouri Governor to discuss political issues relevant to collegiate leaders.
   ▪ Attended Governor's Annual Prayer Breakfast, with guest speaker Jean Carnahan.

Group Leader, Conquering Life's Challenges Academy   **June 2002**
   ▪ Supervised 10 children ages 7 to 9 during summer day camp.
   ▪ Acted as liaison between parents, children, and staff; communicated important information.
   ▪ Helped with meal preparation and enrichment activities.

Word Count: 442

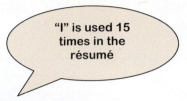

Michael Spencer
714 S. Cherry Street
Rensselaer, IN 47978
PH: (219) 592-9111

Objective

I am seeking a position to further my learning and growth as an employee at a medical office. An internship or seasonal position would be beneficial to me because I wish to continue my education. I prefer a job that allows me to grow as an employee while honing my individual business skills.

Summary

I have excelled in office work that has demanded diligence in computer skill, customer support, and executive decision making. During my time as an employee, I have overcome several challenges and difficulties that have given me a broad knowledge of business procedure and etiquette. I hope to incorporate my talent as a decisive thinker, with the new ideas and tactics I learn, to form a greater understanding of efficient and profitable enterprise.

Skills and Qualifications

- ❖ Proficient with Microsoft Office including Word, Excel, Access, Publisher, and PowerPoint. I am familiar with 10-key entry and type at an average of 70-75 words per minute.
- ❖ Confident in customer relations, daily client communications, and correspondence.
- ❖ Thorough in organizing data and creating appropriate software to allocate and edit that data.
- ❖ Familiar with use of office equipment such as photocopiers, fax machines, postage meters, scales, mass-mailing techniques, printed envelopes, filing systems, Internet, and e-mail.
- ❖ Experienced in analyzing information and incorporating it into a document or report of finding.
- ❖ Worked as an integral part of a team of Realtors who moved $2.9 million in real estate during my time with them.

Work Experience

5/2004 – Present   Lightning Protection Institute   Rensselaer, IN
Executive Assistant
I hold the position of Executive Assistant in a not-for-profit organization involving the lightning protection industry. My responsibilities are creating and maintaining a database of several hundred members and acting as a medium of reference to clients interested in those members. I administer customer relations, many aspects of windows software and its implementation, as well as several forms of media that are distributed daily.

6/2004 – 9/2004   United Country Pinnacle-Realty   Rensselaer, IN
Office Manager
As an Office Manager I ran general business operations and the placement of 6 Realtors in position to communicate and succeed as a team. I was responsible for deadlines being met in all mass mailings and literature; key elements being that I took input from the 6 Realtors, combined the information into an appropriate design, and then I dispersed the literature accordingly. Another duty as an Office Manager was that all phone inquiries traveled through my office where clients were directed to an appropriate representative.

Education

2003 – Present
I am currently a mid-year sophomore at St. Joseph's College striving toward an Associate's Degree in Business Administration and Medical Terminology.

Word Count: 443

Michael Spencer

714 S. Cherry Street
Rensselaer, IN 47978

(219) 592-9111
mspencer@hotmail.net

OBJECTIVE

To obtain an office manager position with a physician practice group.

KEY SKILLS

- Proficient with Microsoft Office including Word, Excel, Access, Publisher, PowerPoint, Paint, 10-key entry, Internet Explorer, and e-mail. Easily edit Microsoft Office software, such as Access and Excel, to pull information from several different sources and compile the data into specifically designed reports.
- Confident in working with clients to solve problems and meet requests. Answered questions and processed information of nearly 20 separate businesses a day.
- Thorough at organizing data for spreadsheets, databases, and other documents.
- Excel in office work that demands diligence in computer skills, customer support, and executive decision making.
- Assisted a team of Realtors© who moved $2.9 million in real estate during time with them.

EDUCATION

Associate of Science in Business Administration & Medical Terminology   April 2008
Saint Joseph's College, Rensselaer, Indiana   GPA 3.16 / 4.0
Relevant coursework to be completed by Summer 2007:

- Medical Terminology (9 hours)
- Computer Applications
- Accounting (9 hours)
- Management Information Systems
- Managerial Communications
- Principles of Marketing
- Principles of Management

WORK EXPERIENCE

Lightning Protection Institute ~ Rensselaer, Indiana   May 2005 – Present
Executive Assistant
Work in an international, not-for-profit organization involving the lightning protection industry. Joined the institute after change in ownership and was charged with task of re-creating all documentation for the new system. Implement and alter information for brochures and other literature, and transfer individual company's information into newly designed database. Provide customer assistance and solve clients' problems by answering questions over the phone, e-mail, or mail.

United Country Pinnacle Realty ~ Rensselaer, Indiana   June 2005 – September 2005
Office Manager
Ran general business operations and directed clients to appropriate real estate agent in order to maximize profit. Met deadlines in all mass mailings and literature; key elements were taking input from the 6 Realtors©, combining the information into an appropriate design, and then dispersing the literature accordingly. Handled all phone inquiries and directed clients to an appropriate representative.

HONORS AND ACTIVITIES

American Marketing Association
SIFE (Students In Free Enterprise)
Ad Ink (advertising club)

Campus Crusade for Christ
- Co-leader on the Servant Team
- Visibility/Technology Team Leader

Word Count: 363

Davis Platt ▪ MS, CSCS, ACE-PT

711 Highland Avenue, Maryville, MO 64468 ▫ 660.528.1670 ▫ Dplatt@hotmail.com

⚱ FOCUS: COMMUNITY HEALTH AND PERSONAL FITNESS ⚱

⚱ KEY CREDENTIALS ⚱

- **Certified Strength and Conditioning Specialist (CSCS)** 2002 – Current
  National Strength and Conditioning Association (NSCA)
- **Pilates Certified Mat Class Instructor** 2002 – Current
- **Precision Cycling Certification**
  Spin Instructor 2002 – Current

- **Jump Stretch Flex-Band Instructor/Distributor** 2002 – Current
- **American Council on Exercise (ACE-PT)**
  Certified Personal Trainer 2000 – Current
- **American Red Cross**
  First Aid and CPR, 1997 – Current
  Lifeguard, 2001 – Current
  AED Certification, 2001 – Current

⚱ PROFESSIONAL EXPERIENCE ⚱

Personal Trainer/Fitness Specialist   *Maryville Community Center (MCC)* ~ Maryville, Missouri   Dec. 2003 – Present
- Provide personal training and workout design for clients ranging in age from 10 – 90. Excel at encouraging individuals at all fitness levels to maximize their potential.
- Design and implement Speed and Agility Camps for local high school and university athletes.
- Teaching Senior Circuit Aerobics, Advanced Aerobics, and Weight Training 101 Class.
- Represent MCC at Health Fairs and promote services to local businesses.

Owner   Northwest Fitness, Maryville, Missouri   Dec. 2003 – Present
- Entrepreneur of Jump Stretch Flex-Band equipment distribution company.
- Design and implement Speed and Agility Camps for local high schools targeting all sports.
- Provide personal training and workout design.

Personal Trainer/Fitness Staff   *HealthWorks Rehab and Fitness*, Morgantown, West Virginia   Aug. 2001 – Dec. 2003
- Performed fitness testing on members – 150 members tested.
- Conducted personal training and designed workouts.
- Organizing Strength and Conditioning Camps for high school athletes.
- Implemented "Precision Cycling" classes for members ages 15 – 60.

Personal Trainer/Wellness Center Supervisor   *Principal Financial Group*, Des Moines, Iowa   Jan. 2001 – Aug. 2001
- Performed fitness testing on members and designed workouts plans (anaerobic and aerobic) to help clients achieve goals.
- Set up and coordinated adult leagues (softball, golf, track, basketball) – with 200 employees involved.

⚱ COACHING/TEACHING EXPERIENCE ⚱

Assistant Football Coach   Maryville High School, Maryville, Missouri   Aug. 2004 – Present
(seasonal)
- Volunteer as Linebacker/Tight End Coach. During 2004 season two players earned 1st team All Conference. Season resulted in first playoff appearance since 1982.

Assistant Football Coach   University High School, Morgantown, West Virginia   Aug. 2001 – Dec. 2003
(seasonal)
- Volunteered time during three seasons to coach linebackers. Appeared in state playoffs all three years.
- Four players earned 1st team All-Conference Linebacker status.

Davis Platt ▪ MS, CSCS, ACE-PT – Page 2

ϒ EDUCATION ϒ

Master of Science Degree in Physical Education ▫ West Virginia University, Morgantown, West Virginia   December 2003
Major: Athletic Coaching Education   Emphasis: Strength and Conditioning   GPA 3.78/4.0
- Graduate Assistant Instructor: PE164 Weight Training & PE265 Principles and Problems of Coaching

Bachelor of Science Degree ▫ Northwest Missouri State University, Maryville, Missouri   December 2000
Double Major: Corporate Wellness and Therapeutic Recreation   GPA 3.52/4.0

Bearcat Varsity Football
- 2000 Second Team All-Conference – Linebacker
- Member of 1998 & 1999 NCAA Division II National Champion Teams
- Varsity Letter Winner, 1997 – 2000

- Academic All-Conference, 1997 – 2000

Northwest Missouri State University Academic
- Presidential Academic Honor Roll, 1999
- "Family of the Year Award," 1998
- Academic Honor Roll, 1997 – 2000

ϒ PROFESSIONAL ORGANIZATIONS ϒ

- National Strength and Conditioning Association (NSCA) 2001 – present
- American Council on Exercise (ACE) 2000 – present
- Health, Physical Education, Dance, and Recreation (HPERD), 1997 – 2000

- Fellowship of Christian Athletes (FCA), 1997 – 2000
- Missouri Club, Letter Winners Organization, 1997 – 2000
- Sigma Phi Epsilon Fraternity, 1996 – 2000

ϒ REFERENCES ϒ

Mr. Brian Espey
Sport Specific Program Coordinator
HealthWorks Rehab and Fitness
9430 Maple Drive
Morgantown, WV 26505
304.599.2514

Mr. Andrew Gerdts
Head Football Coach
Northwest Missouri State University University
Lamkin Activity Center
Maryville, MO 64468
660.562.1300

Dr. Anthony Groumoutis
Professor
School of Physical Education
West Virginia University
Morgantown, WV 26505
304.293.3290 x5236

Mr. Tanner Campbell
Director
Maryville Community Center
140 Country Club Road
Maryville, MO 64468
660.562.2921

Mr. Eric Shelley
Football Defensive Coordinator
High School
991 Price Street
Morgantown, WV 26505
304.288.9925

Mr. Eric Bostwick
Defensive Coordinator
Northwest Missouri State University
Lamkin Activity Center
Maryville, MO 64468
660.562.1780

Word Count: 670

Anna Paige Hughes

Bland format
needed a little work

833 North Congress, Apt. 17, Kansas City, MO 64153, 816-587-3300, Ahughes@umkc.edu

Objectives
- To obtain a pharmacy internship position at Wal-Mart
- Acquire internship hours necessary for Pharm. D. licensure
- To gain personal experience in a pharmacy practice

Work experience
- Pharm Assess - Shawnee Mission, KS - [April, 2003 – present   ]
  Pharm Assess is a pharmacy benefits management and consulting company. Pharm Assess offers many services to pharmacies as well as patients without pharmacy benefits.
  Position: Pharmacy Intern
  Key Responsibilities:
    o Answering customer service calls (i.e. assisting a pharmacy to process a claim, or answering questions that members may have about their benefits).
    o Sending out mailings to pharmacies and members.
    o Database entry.
    o General secretarial duties.
- Osco Drug - Kansas City, MO - [May, 2002 – September, 2003   ]
  Osco Drug is a community pharmacy that provides pharmaceutical care to all aspects within the population, placing a great emphasis on patient conveniences.
  Position: Pharmacy Intern
  Key Responsibilities:
    o Talking with patients and entering all necessary information to fill their prescriptions into a database.
    o Counting tablets and pulling medications from the shelves.
    o Taking prescription transfers and new prescriptions over the phone.
    o Answering patients' questions.
    o General clerk duties.
- Carter's Clinic Pharmacy - Maryville, MO - [August, 1998 – August, 2001/ Summer, 2002   ]
  Carter's Clinic pharmacy is an independently owned and operated
  community pharmacy that strives to deliver the best pharmaceutical care available for the patient in a professional and confidential manner.
  Position: Pharmacy Technician
  Key Responsibilities:
    o Entering prescriptions into a database.
    o Counting tablets and pulling medications from the shelves.
    o Answering phones.
    o General clerk duties.

Education
- Doctor of Pharmacy - University of Missouri at Kansas City [2001 – present   ]

Certifications/ licensures
- Basic cardiac support certification
- Missouri pharmacy internship license
    o License number 2002014986 (expiration date December 31, 2006)

Professional Development
- Proficient in Microsoft Office 2002, medical terminology, pharmacy marketing and management
- Basic understanding of the Spanish language

Word Count: 340

Anna Paige Hughes
Doctor of Pharmacy Candidate
833 North Congress Apt. 17, Kansas City, MO 64153 (816) 587-3300
Ahughes@umkc.edu

OBJECTIVE

- To acquire 750 internship hours necessary for Doctorate of Pharmacy licensure through various pharmaceutical rotation sites

QUALIFICATION STATEMENT

- Five years' experience working in a community pharmacy
- Working knowledge of small and large prescription entry systems
- Solid knowledge base of many prescription insurance plans (Caremark, Express Scripts, partially funded programs, and discount cards)
- Demonstrate excellent time management and organizational skills working in fast-paced environment requiring accuracy

RELATED WORK EXPERIENCE

Pharmacy Intern

Pharmacy Assessments – Shawnee Mission, Kansas   April 2003 – Present
Pharmacy benefits management and consulting company that offers many services to pharmacies as well as patients without pharmacy benefits.
- Answer customer service calls, troubleshoot pharmacy claims, and answer questions that members may have about their benefits
- Send out mailings to pharmacies and members
- Perform database entry
- Complete clerical duties such as creating labels, cover letters, filing papers, and placing office supply orders

Pharmacy Intern

Osco Drug – Kansas City, Missouri   May 2002 – September 2003
Community pharmacy, which provides pharmaceutical care to all aspects within the population placing a great emphasis on patient conveniences.
- Completed HIPAA training program
- Took prescription transfers and new prescriptions over the phone
- Verified prescriptions for completeness and accuracy
- Entered all necessary information to fill a patient's prescription into a database with great attention to detail
- Established and maintained patient profiles
- Pulled medications from the shelves and counted tablets
- Answered patients' questions while expressing empathy and compassion toward patients

Pharmacy Technician

Carter's Clinic Pharmacy – Maryville, Missouri   August 1998 – August 2001, Summer 2002
Independently owned and operated community pharmacy, which strives to deliver the best pharmaceutical care available for the patient in a professional and confidential manner.
- Developed a passion for the field of pharmacy
- Entered all necessary information to fill a patient's prescription into a database with great attention to detail
- Pulled medications from the shelves and counted tablets
- Answered phones, stocked shelves, and took inventory

EDUCATION

Doctor of Pharmacy   May 2006
University of Missouri at Kansas City, Kansas City, Missouri
- Proficient with pharmaceutical software – Lexi-Comp (both online and through hand-held PDA)
- Excellent skills in Microsoft Office – Excel, Outlook, PowerPoint, and Word
- Basic understanding of the Spanish language
- Tuition self-funded through student loans and working part-time during school and full-time in the summers

CERTIFICATIONS/LICENSURES

- Basic cardiac support certification (CPR)
- Registered Pharmacy Intern
- Missouri pharmacy internship license – License number 2002014986   **Word Count: 426**

■ INDUSTRIAL PSYCHOLOGY AND MANAGEMENT

Boston Schneider—Industrial Psychology

Boston's original version needed a facelift, because it was a challenge to read. His transformed résumé does an exceptional job of pulling human resource keywords out of traditional college student jobs and activities.

Allison Anders—Management

At first glance, the next two résumés could be identical twins, but the revised version includes 56 more words, which clarify positions and activities so that transferable skills are included.

James Moore—Management

James was ready to pursue his first internship, but his résumé did not sell his strengths. He hit the weight room and added 226 words to beef up his physique.

Mitch McManaman—Management

Mitch dressed for the occasion (pursuing a recruiting internship) by focusing on leadership activities in his fraternity instead of overdescribing a previous position in retail.

Keywords for Industrial Psychology and Management

Industry Jargon			
• Administer surveys	• Employee	• Interview	• Productivity
• Affirmative Action	• Satisfaction surveys	• Inventory control	• Program development
• Annual salary	• Employee/labor relations	• Knowledge management	• Project coordination
• Background checks	• Entrepreneur	• Labor laws	• Project management
• Benchmarking	• Event management	• Leadership training	• Public relations
• Benefits	• Event planning	• Logistics	• Quality control
• Compensation	• Family Medical	• Manufacturing	• Recruiting
• Confidential manner	Leave Act (FMLA)	• Negotiations	• Safety/Security
• Consolidated	• Filed insurance	• Nonprofit	• Scheduling
Ombius	claims	• Occupational Safety and	• Selection
Reconciliation Act	• Forecasting	Health Organization	• Staffing
(COBRA)	• Hired/terminated	(OSHA)	• Total quality
• Decision-making	• Human resource	• Operations management	management (TQM)
authority	• Human Resource	• Orientation	• Training
• Department policy	Information System	• Performance	• Workers'
manual	(HRIS)	evaluations/review	Compensation
• Discipline	• I-9	• Personnel	
• Diversity	• Insurance (health,	• Presentations	
• Employee newsletter	dental, life, disability)	• Production management	
• Employee orientation	• Internal employee		
and tours	communications		

Positions—Sought, Held, or Reported To

- Associate
- Benefits Specialist
- Branch Manager
- Committee Chair
- Director of Recruiting
- Generalist
- Health and Safety Manager
- Human Resource Assistant
- Human Resource Specialist
- Internship
- Liaison
- Manager
- Mediator

- Payroll Supervisor
- Peer Advisor
- Personnel Administrator
- President/Vice President
- Recruitment Chair
- Resident Assistant
- Section Manager
- Standard Committee
- Student Ambassador
- Supervisor
- Supplemental Instructor
- Team Captain
- Team Leader
- Trainer

Personality Traits

- Accountable/dependable
- Active listener
- Adaptable/flexible
- Budget-conscious
- Caring
- Creative
- Detail oriented
- Diplomatic
- Dynamic
- Enjoys challenges
- Ethical/honest
- Facilitator
- Handle confidential information
- Interpersonal skills
- Leadership abilities
- Liaison
- Mediator
- Multitasker

- Organized
- Patient
- People oriented
- Persuasive
- Positive attitude
- Problem solver
- Professional
- Project oriented
- Quick learner
- Resourceful
- Sensitive to others
- Success driven
- Tactful
- Team builder
- Time manager
- Troubleshooter
- Work well under pressure

Computer Skills

- Dreamweaver
- FrontPage
- Microsoft Access
- Microsoft Excel
- Microsoft Outlook
- Microsoft PowerPoint
- Microsoft Project
- Microsoft Publisher
- Microsoft Word
- Oracle
- PeopleSoft
- Quatro Pro
- Quicken
- Visio
- Windows OS
- WordPerfect

Professional Associations

- DECA
- Delta Mu Delta (business honor society)
- Job Services Employee Committee
- Pi Beta Alpha
- Society of Human Resource Management (SHRM)
- Students In Free Enterprise (SIFE)

Degrees and Certifications

- Bachelor of Science in Business Management
- Bachelor of Science in Industrial Management or Industrial Psychology Industrial
- Master in Business Administration
- Professional Human Resource Certification (PHR)
- Accounting

- Business Law
- Finance
- Fundamentals of Management
- Human Resource Management
- Marketing
- Organizational Theory Production and Operations Management

Boston Schneider

115 N College Dr. # 97, Iowa City, IA 59034
(319) 674-8260
s202626@universityia.edu

Lacks organization, structure, and effective use of white space

Objective Office assistant position in IIC office
Education
University of Iowa, Iowa City, Iowa
Bachelor of Science, Industrial Psychology, expected graduation December 2006   GPA 4.0/4.0

University Activities
Society of Human Resource Management   Fall 2004–Spring 2005
  Attending meetings that invite Human Resource Managers to optimize knowledge and career in HRM.
Chinese Student Association Secretary   Spring 2004–Fall 2004
                      Vice President   Spring 2005
  Maintaining continuous communication among members, and recruiting new members for the organization
International Student Organization   Spring 2003–Spring 2005
  Actively participated in decoration group for ISO dinner, and commitment to float for homecoming parade
Scholarship
CSA scholarship   Spring 2004
Employment
August 2003–Present   Server   Aramark   Iowa City, Iowa
  • Take orders from patrons.
  • Maintain quality services.
  • Responsible for clean serving environment.
March 2002–December 2002   Part-time position   Seattle's Best Coffee   Fukuoka, Japan
  • Accountable for accurate balance of cash register.
  • Prepared different flavors of coffee dairy.
  • Provided quality services to customers (i.e., explain differences among a variety of coffee beans from different countries).
  • Responsible for giving employees instructions on specific orders.
January 2002–March 2002   Caterer   Seahawk Hotel   Fukuoka, Japan
  • Provided wedding receptions to groups of 50–100 patrons.
  • Responsible for appropriate meal preparation for children and elderly guests.
  • Trained new colleagues in proper meal preparation.
December 2001–January 2002   Telephone operator Kuroneko home-delivery service center   Fukuoka, Japan
  • Properly took orders from customers.
  • Answered their inquiries about their orders (time delivered).
  • Took complaints from customers and corresponded with delivery personnel.
August 2000–July 2001   Cashier   Mr.MaX   Fukuoka, Japan
  • Accurate accounting of cash balances daily.
  • Cordially responded to top telephone inquiries.
  • Promptly resolved returned items/goods.
Community Services
1999–2001   Provided "special days" for handicapped children and put together a cultural festival for handicapped children
2004   Adopt-A-Highway program
Language Fluency: Japanese and English
Computer Skills: Internet and Microsoft Office 2000 (Word, Excel, PowerPoint, and Access)

Word Count: 321

Boston Schneider

115 N. College Dr. # 97, Iowa City, IA 59034
(319) 674-8260
s202626@universityia.edu

Revamped
layout works

OBJECTIVE

To obtain a Human Resource internship at Tribune Company.

EDUCATION

Bachelor of Science in Industrial Psychology   **December 2006**
University of Iowa   Iowa City, Iowa   **Major GPA: 4.0/4.0**   **Overall GPA: 3.96/4.00**
Scholarships ~ University of IA Platinum Regents Scholarship, CSA Scholarship, ISO Scholarship
Presidential Honor Roll (4.0–5 semesters) Academic Honor Roll (3.5 and above–1 semester)
Computer Skills: Microsoft (Word, Excel, Access, PowerPoint) and Internet Explorer
Related course work to Human Resource to be completed by Summer 2006

Human Resource Management	Using Computers	Negotiations
Managerial Communications	Organizational Theory	Industrial Psychology

EMPLOYMENT

Server   Aramark   Iowa City, Iowa   August 2003–Present
Interact with and serve 80–100 customers from diverse backgrounds. Trusted to train five new colleagues. Take orders from patrons. Maintain excellent service. Responsible for clean serving environment. Learning to communicate and work with diverse group of employees.

Server   Seattle's Best Coffee   Harlan, Iowa   March 2002–December 2002
Fast-paced environment required multitasking skills (cashiering, taking orders, preparing coffee specialty drinks). Accountable for accurate balance of cash register. Provided quality services to customers through explaining differences among variety of coffee beans from different countries. Responsible for giving employees instructions on specific orders.

Telephone Operator   Home-Delivery Service   Harlan, Iowa   December 2001–January 2002
Properly took orders from customers. Answered inquiries about orders. Investigated situations involving lost or late deliveries, communicated with delivery personnel to resolve matters, and assured customers the situation would be resolved.

Cashier/Customer Service Mr.MaX   Harlan, Iowa   August 2000–July 2001
Operated register and assisted customers by checking out items. Responsible for accurate accounting of cash balances daily. Cordially responded to telephone inquiries. Promptly processed returned items/goods.

HONORS AND ACTIVITIES

Society of Human Resource Management (Fall 2004–Present)

International Student Association (Spring 2003–Present)
- Vice President - Recruit new members by organizing welcome party and encouraging members to bring new students to the meetings. Coordinate annual dinners and fund-raising activities. Interact with the director of International Intercultural Affairs Office. Persuading local businesses to sponsor annual dinner that serves 150. Advertise for events using the campus paper, flyers, mass e-mailing, and word of mouth.
- Secretary - Maintained continuous communication among 25 members through prompt e-mails announcing meetings. Updated member roster. Kept track of participation point system used to calculate student awards.

PROFESSIONAL PORTFOLIO AVAILABLE

Word Count: 387

Allison Anders

5000 Thorn St., Cambridge, MA 00138 (619) 875-6150   allisonanders@yahoo.com

----

OBJECTIVE

To obtain a job as Office Manager at the Lower Manhattan Cultural Council.

EDUCATION

Harvard University   Cambridge, MA   August 2004 – Present
Bachelor of Science in Business Management   December 2008
30% of educational funding provided by scholarships and working part-time while attending
school full-time.

Job descriptions weak

WORK EXPERIENCE

Desk Manager ~ Harvard Residential Life Department, Cambridge, MA   August 2005 – Present
- Prepare and deliver training for new desk employees. Create work schedule for 15
  employees. Maintain petty cash. Order and stock supplies. Answer and direct phone
  calls.

Server ~ Harvard Campus Dinning, Cambridge, MA   August 2004 – March 2005
- Prepared and delivered food in a courteous and timely manner. Bused tables after guests
  were done. Operated large automatic dishwasher.

House Keeping ~ Boston Inn, Boston, MA   June 2004 – August 2004
- Preformed daily cleaning duties such as changing sheets, vacuuming, and bathroom
  sanitation. Completed reservation process over phone and in person. Checked guests
  into their rooms. Delivered additional goods to ensure comfort. Helped maintain income
  summary on a daily and monthly level.

Baker ~ Chesapeake Bagel Bakery, Boston, MA   March 2002 – Present
- Mix ingredients in a mixer capable of holding 200 pounds of flour to create bagel dough
  from scratch. Use former to produce over 260 bagels per batch. On average complete
  three batches per shift. Use 500 degree, five-shelf carousel oven to bake bagels. Operate
  register and make change for customers. Serve customers by preparing food and
  gourmet coffee items. Complete several cleaning duties. Organize delivery invoices. Help
  proofread schedule for errors. Job offered back for breaks.

LEADERSHIP ACTIVITIES

- Delta Zeta – Pledge class pep-chair, Continuous Open Bid chair, Judiciary Board chair,
  Homecoming float chair.
- Hall council – Floor representative, Disciplinary Committee member, Publicity Committee
  member, Birthday Recognition Committee.
- Bible School teacher – Volunteer summers to teach five-year-olds.
- MA State Games Volunteer – Serve as field marshal for soccer.

HONORS AND ACHIEVEMENTS

- Shelter Insurance Scholarship
- Residential Life Desk Manager Scholarship
- Winner of Chesapeake Bagel Top Solicited Sales Award
- Junior Varsity Soccer Captain two years
- Varsity Co-Captain one year

White space not effectively used

Word Count: 352

Allison Anders

5000 Thorn St., Cambridge, MA 00138 (619) 875-6150   allisonanders@yahoo.com

OBJECTIVE

To obtain a Summer 2004 marketing/communications internship with CPRi.

EDUCATION

Bachelor of Science Degree with majors in Business Management and Marketing   *December 2008*
Harvard University   *Cambridge, Massachusetts*
- 50% of educational funding provided by scholarships and working 20 hours per week; attending school full-time.
- Computer skills include Microsoft Office, Internet, and e-mail.

WORK EXPERIENCE

Desk Manager ~ Harvard Residential Life Department, Cambridge, Massachusetts   August 2005 – Present
- Prepare and execute interactive training sessions demonstrating correct procedure for completing paperwork. Create and maintain work schedule for 14 employees. Maintain petty cash funds of $300. Maintain a detailed key inventory for over 800 keys. Order and stock supplies such as stamps, envelopes, light bulbs, office supplies, and forms. Answer and direct phone calls. Politely and professionally assist residents with their inquiries.

Server ~ Harvard Campus Dining, Cambridge, Massachusetts   August 2004 – March 2005
- Prepared and delivered food in a courteous and timely manner. Bused tables after guests were finished. Operated large automatic dishwasher.

Reservations / Housekeeping ~ Boston Inn, Boston, Massachusetts   June 2004 – August 2004
- Completed reservation process over phone and in person. Checked guests into their rooms. Helped maintain income summary reports on a daily and monthly level that required extreme attention to detail. Performed daily cleaning duties such as changing sheets, vacuuming, and bathroom sanitation.

Baker ~ Chesapeake Bagel Bakery, Boston, Massachusetts   March 2002 – Present
- Complete three batches of 260 bagels per shift. Operate register and make change for customers. Serve several customers at a time by preparing food and gourmet coffee items in a timely fashion. Organize delivery invoices. Help proofread weekly schedule for errors.

LEADERSHIP ACTIVITIES

- Delta Zeta – Pledge class pep-Chair, Continuous Open Bid Chair, Judiciary Board Chair, Homecoming Float Chair, Team Leadership Conference participant, Martin Luther King Day of Service participant, volunteer at Bristol Manor and Children's Center
- Hall Council – Floor Representative, Disciplinary Committee member, Publicity Committee member, Birthday Recognition Committee Chair
- Bible School teacher – Volunteer summers to teach five-year-olds
- Show-Me State Games volunteer – Served as field marshal for soccer games, registered teams, and delivered result card

HONORS AND ACHIEVEMENTS

- Shelter Insurance Foundation Scholarship
- Residential Life Desk Manager Scholarship
- Winner of Chesapeake Bagel Top Solicited Sales Award
- Winner of Delta Zeta "Social Butterfly" Award

- Selected to Participate in World Youth Day Pilgrimage
- 2005 – 2006 Franken Staff Positive Leader

Word Count: 408

James Moore

E-mail: jmoore@something.com

Current Address
337 Berry Drive
Abilene, TX 39744
(818) 347-1197

Permanent Address
904 Staton Boulevard
Austin, TX 39677
(574) 193-2212

Objective: To obtain a full-time position at Six Flags.

Education: Abilene Christian University, anticipated Graduation in April 2008
Bachelor of Science
Major: Business Management and Marketing

Related Coursework:
Managerial Communications   Accounting I & II
Economics I & II   Managerial Process and Behavior
Principals of Marketing   Principals of Management

Typos are not cool!

Personal Profile:
- Take initiative
- Work well without being continuously monitored
- Level-headed
- Problem solver

Work Experience:
- Hannibal Country Club, May 2004–Present
    Complete Customer Services
        *Assure comfort   *Waiter
        *Complete satisfaction   *Bus boy
- Hannibal Concrete Products, May 2004–August 2004
        *Responsible for preparing the molds.
- Riverview Café, May 2003–March 2004
        *Responsible for managing a shift of bus boys.

Unclear duties

Activities: Campus Crusade for Christ
Fellowship of Christian Athletes
Abilene Men's Club Soccer Team
Brush Volunteer

Word Count: 156

James Moore

Address: 337 Berry Drive, Abilene, TX 39744 – 818-347-1197
E-mail: jmoore@something.com

OBJECTIVE

To obtain a summer internship in the area of Business Management at Six Flags.

EDUCATION

Bachelor of Science with major in Business Management   *April 2007*
Abilene Christian University, Abilene, Texas   GPA 3.10
  • Computer Software: Microsoft Word, Excel, PowerPoint, Works

Related course work to be completed by Summer 2006

Management:	Principles of Management	Negotiations
	Managerial Communications	Managerial Processes and Behavior
	Organizational Theory and Behavior	Human Resource Management
Business:	Economics I & II	Accounting I & II
	Entrepreneurship	Business Law
	Principles of Marketing	

WORK EXPERIENCE

Camp Counselor   **Ormond Beach Community Center**   Abilene, Texas   June 2005–Aug. 2005
Interacted and supervised 30 ten- to twelve-year-olds from diverse backgrounds throughout the day and assisted with the multiple games they participated in. Gained experience taking initiative and making decisions when situations would arise and prompt action was required.

Pool Service   **Quality Pools, Inc.**   Abilene, Texas   May 2005–June 2005
Traveled throughout Abilene cleaning and servicing pools as a team of two. Learned how to work well without being constantly monitored by a supervisor. Accountable for making sure the customer was pleased when service was complete.

Bus Boy/Pool Worker   **Hannibal Country Club**   Hannibal, Texas   May 2004–Dec. 2005
Worked in a fast-paced environment that required multiple tasks to be completed quickly. Made sure all tables in the restaurant were cleared, cleaned, and set in a respectable manner. Developed problem-solving skills dealing with unplanned situations. Operated the concession stand at the pool. Developed skills pleasing upscale clientele.

Concrete Worker   **Hannibal Concrete Products**   Hannibal, Texas   May 2004–Aug. 2004
Stripped, cleaned, and prepared molds for the concrete with a team of 10. Worked under a time schedule that helped develop excellent teamwork skills.

Bus Boy   **Riverview Café**   Hannibal, Texas   May 2003–Aug. 2003
Interacted with 200–300 customers daily (roughly half were tourists). Similar responsibilities of the job at the Country Club. Advised customers about what they may want to see or the locations of places throughout the town. Learned how to relate to people while serving them.

ACTIVITIES

❑ Campus Crusade for Christ   ❑ Navigators
    -Leader on the Servant Team   ❑ Club Soccer Team
    -Social-event team   ❑ Delta Mu Delta
❑ BRUSH Volunteer   (Top 20% of Business Students)

Word Count: 382

Mitch McManaman

3008 E. Berry Street, Los Angeles, CA 80931 / (415) 396-7703
Mmcmanaman@msn.net

(callout: Shading is too dark for the section headings)

OBJECTIVE

To obtain a summer internship as recruiting manager at Marriott's Resort.

EDUCATION

- Bachelor of Science in Business Management and Marketing   May 2008
  ~ University of Southern California, Los Angeles, California.   GPA 3.5/4.0

WORK EXPERIENCE

American Eagle   Los Angeles, CA   Nov. 2003–Feb. 2005
- Sales Representative

  (callout: Changing font size allows for 155 more words)

  Organized backroom to increase availability of products. While in between stock managers, had total control of operations in stockroom. Controlled all organization, incoming stock, and employment stock problems during that time. Increased the organization and employee accessibility of stockroom. In charge of floor changes, making them quicker and more appealing to customers. Worked with customers to complete transactions while maintaining high customer satisfaction. Made decision to comply with customer decisions based on opinions of customer's integrity. Worked the register and sales floor. For multiple weeks was the top employee in credit card registrations, which is the salesperson's main focus. Position dealt largely with sales, loss prevention, and conflict management. Through raises over the working term became the highest paid nonmanager at the location.

Bakers Square Restaurant   Los Angeles, CA   Aug. 2002–Aug. 2004
- Server

  Served customers, bused, and seated tables. Dealt with customer service and sales.

Calypso 968   Los Angeles, CA   Nov. 2001–Feb. 2002
- Salesperson

  Worked the cash register for an upstart art and antique business. Involved in sales, stock, customer service, and loss prevention. Dealt with customer's returns, exchanges, and satisfaction.

HONORS AND ACTIVITIES

- American Marketing Association
  VP of Finance
- Sigma Phi Epsilon Social Fraternity
  Outstanding New Member
  VP of Recruitment
  Scholarship Chair
  Intramural Chair
  Pledge Class President
- Team Leadership

  (callout: Expand as it relates to target)

- Community Service
  Retirement Home (40 hrs.)
  Humane Society (20 hrs.)
  Other (20 hrs.)
- Emerging Leader Award
- Academic Achievement Scholarship
- Dean's List (3.5–4.0)
- President's List (4.0)

Word Count: 300

Mitch McManaman

3008 E. Berry Street, Los Angeles, CA 80931
(415) 396-7703 / Mmcmanaman@msn.net

OBJECTIVE

To obtain a summer internship as recruiting manager at Marriott Resort.

EDUCATION

Bachelor of Science degree; double major in Business Management and Marketing   May 2008
University of Southern California, Los Angeles, California   GPA 3.5/4.0
- **Classes completed by Spring 2006:**
  - ~ Management Process and Behavior   ~ Managerial Communications
  - ~ Accounting I & II   ~ Principles of Marketing
- Plan to study abroad and have internship in Europe during the spring and summer semesters of 2007
- Computer Skills: Microsoft Word, Excel, Publisher, PowerPoint, Internet Explorer

Expand descriptions of leadership if relevant to the position

RELATED EXPERIENCE

Sigma Phi Epsilon Social Fraternity   Los Angeles, California
- **Vice President of Recruitment**   Apr. 2004 – Present
Managed five members during recruitment and developed strategies to improve the year-round recruitment for the fraternity. Planned and developed flyers for rush events. Designed rush shirts for the chapter and sold them to other chapters for a fund-raiser. Elected as one of the seven executive members in the fraternity. Provided input dealing with disciplinary issues and future plans. Delegated tasks while maintaining control.
- **Scholarship Chair**   Apr. 2004 – Sept. 2004
Facilitated two scholarship awards. Sent letters to potential candidates, then narrowed down the applicants. Headed and coordinated the interviewing and selection process of the final 10 candidates.

American Eagle Outfitters   Los Angeles, California
- **Stockroom Manager**   Nov. 2004 – Feb. 2005
Controlled all organization, incoming stock, and employment stock problems. Improved the organization and employee accessibility of stockroom. In charge of facilitating floor changes. Delegated tasks between two stockroom employees.
- **Returns and Exchanges**   Feb. 2004 – Nov. 2005
Worked with customers to complete transactions while maintaining high customer satisfaction. Made decision to comply with store policy based on opinions of customer's integrity.
- **Salesperson**   Nov. 2003 – Nov. 2004
Worked the register and sales floor. For 18 weeks was the top employee in credit card registrations. Position dealt largely with sales and loss prevention. Through raises over the year, became the highest paid nonmanager at the location.

Bakers Square Restaurant   Los Angeles, California
- **Server**   Aug. 2002 – Aug. 2004
Seated and served customers and cleared tables. Served up to 100 customers in a shift.

HONORS AND ACTIVITIES

- American Marketing Association
  VP of Finance
- Sigma Phi Epsilon Social Fraternity
  Outstanding New Member
  Intramural Chair
  Pledge Class President
- Student Senate

- Team Leadership
  Emerging Leader Award
- Community Service (per year)
  Retirement Home (40 hrs)
  Humane Society (20 hrs)
- Academic Achievement Scholarship
- President's List (4.0) 1 semester

Word Count: 420

■ MARKETING, MERCHANDISING, AND PUBLIC RELATIONS

Andrea Davidson—Marketing
At initial glance, Andrea's résumé may have made a good first impression, but upon closer review, her shallow work experience descriptions would easily be spotted.

Andy Paxton—Marketing
Any good fashion consultant will tell you that fit is everything. Andy had added skills and experience, so his original size (résumé format) could not accommodate all his added information.

Angelo Rodriquez—Marketing
Angelo added an amazing 196 words to his updated résumé. His after version is packed full of keywords and well-crafted descriptions focusing on transferable skills.

Caroline Morley—Marketing
Caroline possessed a great deal of targeted experience to offer, but the first impression was more that of a wallflower than that of the life of the party. Her revised format and clarified descriptions will help her résumé stand out as the life of the party.

Teri Carlson—Merchandising
Subtle format changes really enhance the readability and visual appeal of the after version. Too many short sections at the top of her résumé were prohibiting the reader from paying attention to one of her most impressive attributes—an impressive position as a technical writer.

Lynette Johnson—Public Relations
Lynette did an excellent job of branding herself by targeting her highlight of skills to meet Starlight Theatre's needs.

Keywords for Marketing, Merchandising, and Public Relations

Positions—Sought, Held, or Reported To		Degrees and Certifications	Professional Associations
• Account Manager	• Internship	• Bachelor of Science in Advertising, Marketing, or Public Relations	• American Marketing Association (AMA)
• Administrative Assistant	• Peer Advisor	• Bachelor of Science in Merchandising	• ASID
• Ambassador	• Planning Clerk	• Minor in Business	• Delta Epsilon Chi
• Assistant	• Recruitment Chair		• Fashion Group International
• Buyer	• Sales Manager		• National Agri-Marketing Association (NAMA)
• Buyer Assistant	• Sales Associate		• Pi Beta Alpha
• Consultant	• Sales Representative		• Students In Free Enterprise (SIFE)
• Creative Director	• Special Events Coordinator		• WIM Conference
• Customer Service Representative	• Store Assistant		
• Director of Marketing	• Store Manager		
• Distributor	• Team Leader		
• Event planner	• Visual Merchandising		
• Fund-Raiser			

Personality Traits		**Computer Skills**
• Accountable/ dependable • Active listener • Budget conscious • Creative • Deadline conscious • Dedicated • Detail oriented • Energetic • Ethical/honest • Eye for fashion • Flexible • Hardworking	• Leadership abilities • Organized • Persuasive • Professional • Project oriented • Quick learner • Responsible • Self-motivator • Success driven • Team player • Time manager • Work well under pressure	• Adobe PhotoShop • Computer-aided design (CAD) • Illustrator • Internet Explorer • Microsoft Access • Microsoft Excel • Microsoft Outlook • Microsoft PowerPoint • Microsoft Publisher • Microsoft Word • PageMaker • Quark • Windows OS • WordPerfect

Industry Jargon

- Advertising
- Brand
- Brochures
- Budget planning
- Campaign
- College recruiting
- Commission
- Convention planning
- Corporate media programs
- Creative writing
- Crisis communication
- Customer service/ satisfaction
- Demographics
- Department stores
- Direct mail marketing
- Displays/display case
- Distribution

- E-commerce
- Event planning
- Floor planning
- Focus group
- Forecasting
- Fund-raising
- Guerilla marketing
- Internet marketing
- Inventory control
- Leadership training
- Logistics
- Loss prevention
- Market analysis/research
- Market segmentation
- Marketing
- Marketing mix
- Media relations
- Meeting planning
- Negotiations
- Newsletters
- Niche markets
- Plan-o-grams

- Point of Purchase (POP)
- Point of Sale (POS)
- Political campaigns
- Positioning
- Presentation
- Press releases
- Price
- Pricing
- Print advertising
- Process inventory
- Project planning
- Promotions
- Propaganda
- Psychographics
- Public relations campaigns
- Public speaking
- Publicity events
- Purchasing
- Racetrack
- Recruiting
- Referrals
- Relationship building

- Relationship marketing
- Retail
- Sales
- Schematics
- Speaker skills
- Specialty stores
- Sports marketing
- Stock
- Store fixtures
- Strategic planning
- Tagline
- Target market
- Telemarketing
- Theft reduction/ shrinkage
- Trade shows
- Training
- Vendors
- Visual merchandising
- Web marketing
- Web pages
- Writing and editing

Andrea Davidson

606 Highway 132
North Adams, VT 36404

616-477-3246
aduncan@mailnet.com

OBJECTIVE

o   Receptionist and Cashier for Vic Auto Plaza

EDUCATION

o   Bachelor of Science, Double Major: Business Management / Marketing   - April 2008
o   Southern Vermont College, Bennington, VT   - GPA 3.75
     100% of educational expenses self-funded through scholarships and working 10 to 15 hours per
     week.

WORK EXPERIENCE

Weak position descriptions

Orientation and Transfer Affairs   Southern Vermont College, Bennington, VT   August 2005
                                                                                     to present

Office Assistant
Answer phones, take messages, help with coordinating plans for orientation and transfer
programs, produce documents, produce and send monthly newsletters, and produce and record
survey information.

Blockbuster Video   North Adams, VT   March 2005 to
                                                                   November 2005

Customer Service Representative
Cashier, answer phones, count inventory, help customers with selections, sell promotions, and work
towards satisfactory evaluations.

Dairy Queen Brazier   North Adams, VT   March 2002 to
                                                                   September 2003

Cashier and Server
Cashier, train employees, take specialty orders, clean kitchen and seating area, prepare orders.

KEY SKILLS

COMPUTER SKILLS
Microsoft Software: Word, Excel, Access, Outlook, PowerPoint, Publisher, and Works
Other: PrintShop, AOL Press, Internet Explorer, and typing
OTHER SKILLS
Auto sales experience through family-owned dealership, Spanish skills, and message taking

HONORS AND ACTIVITIES

- Presidential Scholarship valid
  2004–2008
- Beatty Scholarship
  (top 10% of graduating class)
- Vermont Cheerleading Scholarship

- Sigma Pi Sigma Honor Society for
  Presidential Scholars
- American Marketing Association
- Named to National Society of Collegiate
  Scholars

Word Count: 225

Andrea Davidson

606 Highway 132
North Adams, VT 36404

616-477-3246
aduncan@mailnet.com

OBJECTIVE

To apply experience gained through our family-owned dealership to a receptionist and cashier position at Vic Auto.

EDUCATION

Bachelor of Science, Double Major: Business Management / Marketing, Spanish minor
Southern Vermont College, Bennington, Vermont
100% of educational expenses self-funded through academic scholarships and working 10 hours per week

April 2008
GPA 3.75 / 4.0

WORK EXPERIENCE

Orientation and Transfer Affairs   *Southern Vermont College, Bennington, Vermont*
Office Assistant

August 2005
to present

- Answer phones and either provide information or direct caller to appropriate personnel
- Assist with plans for orientation and transfer for approximately 200 to 300 students each semester by scheduling programs and advisement meetings with 60 faculty
- Develop course-by-course transfer documents requiring attention to detail
- Update articulation agreements with transferable credits at various institutions
- Create and send monthly newsletters to 300 students
- Interpret and record survey information to improve service to students
- Obtaining important filing, message recording, and appointment scheduling skills

Blockbuster Video   *North Adams, Vermont*
Customer Service Representative

March 2005 to
November 2005

- Assisted customers with selections and checkout procedure
- Developed persuasive sales techniques through recommending in-store promotions
- Achieved superior evaluations based on customer service and sales ability

Dairy Queen Brazier   *North Adams, Vermont*
Cashier and Server

March 2002 to
September 2003

- Promoted excellent customer service through sales and employee training
- Trained 3 to 5 employees on cashiering, cleaning, and product preparation
- Recorded and produced specialty cake orders in compliance with customer requests

COMPUTER SKILLS

Microsoft (Word, Excel, Access, Outlook, PowerPoint, Publisher, and Works)

AOL Press, PrintShop, QuickBooks, and Internet Explorer

HONORS AND ACTIVITIES

- Presidential Scholarship
  (2004–present) – only 10 awarded annually
- Beattie Scholarship
  (top 10% of graduating class)
- Vermont Cheerleading Scholarship
  (for leadership and academics)
- Selected as Peer Advisor to Freshman Seminar Class

- Dean's Honor Roll
  (GPA 3.5 or higher)
- Sigma Pi Sigma Honor Society
  (GPA 3.5 or higher)
- American Marketing Association
  (2-year member)
- Named to National Society of Collegiate Scholars – mentoring program

Word Count: 335

(778) 562-5190
301 North Street
Chapel Hill, NC 27599
Paxton@any.com

Andy L. Paxton

Objective   Obtain a position in the areas of Management, Customer Satisfaction, or Human Resources

Experience   March 2002 – Present   First National Bank & Trust   Durham, NC

Teller II
- Process customer transactions in a timely, efficient manner.
- Establish a relationship with frequent visitors to the bank.
- Assist customers in person and on the phone with questions about their accounts.
- Maintain security, sales, and operational standards established by the bank.

Nov. 2002 – Present   University of North Carolina   Chapel Hill, NC

Office Assistant – Vice President for Finance & Support Services
- Greet visitors and direct phone calls to the appropriate individual.
- Work closely with other staff members on various projects.
- Develop spreadsheets to track various university expenditures (Utility, Travel, etc.)
- Complete credit applications and supply vendors with required tax information.
- Assist in production and update of various operations manuals and presentations (Finance Policy & Procedures, Residential Life Master Plan, etc.)
- Student Employee of the Year finalist, received Outstanding Award for Reliability

(Format and font size wastes space)

2000 – 2004   Wal-Mart Stores Inc.   Durham, NC

Customer Service Representative
- Assist customers with returns and exchanges.
- Dealt with customers with concerns regarding the store.
- 4-Star Cashier Award for excellence in customer service.

Education   University of North Carolina, Chapel Hill, NC
- Double major in Marketing and Management
- Cumulative GPA 3.97   Major GPA 4.00
- Anticipated Graduation Date – May 2006

(Education section belongs before experience)

Activities & Honors

President's Honor Roll – 5 Semesters, Academic Honor Roll – 1 Semester
American Society for Quality – Secretary
Alpha Chi – Honor society for top 10% of juniors & seniors
Delta Mu Delta – Business honor society
Phi Eta Sigma – Outstanding freshman honor society

Computer Skills

Windows 98, Windows 2000, Windows XP, Office 97, Office 2000, Office XP, Adobe PageMaker, Adobe Photoshop, Netscape Navigator, Internet Explorer

Word Count: 305

(778) 562-5190
301 North St.
Chapel Hill, NC 27599
Paxton@any.com

Andy L. Paxton

OBJECTIVE

To obtain a Retail Management Trainee position with Walgreens.

PROFILE

Profile sells applicant well

- Outstanding skills in customer relations, communication, and problem solving
- Project self-confidence, authority, and enthusiasm leading projects
- Conducted extensive, successful consulting projects for 2 businesses while in college
- Developed word processing, spreadsheet, database, and presentation software skills
- Work to pay living expenses while maintaining excellent GPA

EDUCATION

Bachelor of Science, Double Major in Marketing and Management   **May 2006**
University of North Carolina – Chapel Hill, North Carolina   GPA 3.97
- Scored in 93rd percentile on Academic Profile test
- Prepared and interpreted extensive student employee satisfaction research for the office of Human Resources
- Developed successful strategic marketing plan for Bateman Photography in Chapel Hill, NC
- Select Honors: President's Honor Roll (6 semesters), National Dean's List (2 years), Academic Honor Roll (1 semester)

WORK EXPERIENCE

Office Assistant, Vice President for Finance and Support Services   **November 2002 – Present**
University of North Carolina ~ Chapel Hill, North Carolina
Greet office visitors and field phone calls for Vice President. Participate in interviewing, hiring, and training student employees. Handle highly confidential University/employee information. Assist in production and update of operations manuals and presentations (Finance Policy & Procedures, Residential Life Master Plan, Financial Improvement Team Yearly Report, etc.). Develop spreadsheets to track University expenditures. Process vendor invoices to ensure timely payment. Assumed job responsibilities of full-time accounting employee for 2 months. Universitywide *Student Employee of the Year* finalist, 2005; received *Outstanding Award for Reliability,* 2005.

Teller II   **March 2002 – Present**
First National Bank & Trust Company ~ Durham, North Carolina
Process customer deposit and loan transactions in an efficient manner while maintaining attention to detail. Assist teller staff with complex transactions and questions. Communicate with customers in person and on the phone with inquiries regarding their accounts while establishing relationships with frequent visitors to the bank. Market bank products to customers. Preserve customer confidentiality while following federal banking guidelines. Received 6 *Applause-O-Grams* for outstanding service from colleagues and promoted to Teller II after 6 months. Asked to continue employment over breaks and summers.

Customer Service Representative   **August 2000 – March 2002**
Wal-Mart Stores Inc. ~ Durham, North Carolina
Assisted customers with returns and exchanges and concerns or comments regarding the store. *4-Star Cashier Award* for excellence in customer service March 2001.

ACTIVITIES & HONORS

American Society for Quality – Secretary
Delta Mu Delta – Top 20% of business majors
Academic Profile Test Scholarship

Alpha Chi – Honor society for top 10% of juniors and seniors
Phi Eta Sigma – Outstanding freshman honor society
Future Business Leaders of America – National Competitor

COMPUTER SKILLS

Windows	Access	Novell GroupWise	Internet Explorer	Kirchman Bankway
Word	PowerPoint	PageMaker	Netscape Navigator	Intracheck
Excel	Outlook	PhotoShop	Lotus 123	Synergy

Word Count: 453

Angelo Rodriquez

Present Address: 600 E. 5th St., Holland, MI 89057   (316) 592-5280
E-Mail Address: Arodriquez@hope.edu

Pre-internship résumé focuses on coursework

OBJECTIVE   Sports Marketing & Management Internship

Vague

EDUCATION

Bachelor of Science, Double Major: Business Management and Marketing   December 2005
Hope College, Holland, MI
Relevant coursework to be completed by Summer 2004

Management Principles	Managerial Comm.	Statistics & Finite
HR Management	Marketing Principles	Accounting (I & II)
Org. Theory & Behavior	Management Info. Systems	Economics (I & II)

RELATED EXPERIENCE

Construction Materials Delivery   Summer 2003
Rew Materials ~ Hamilton, Michigan
- Delivered sheetrock, insulation, etc. to construction sites by truck
- Worked 40 to 70 hours a week in the summer
- Maintained delivery log verifying material delivered and miles traveled
- Lifted and carried heavy materials for deliveries
- Developed ability to pay attention to detail

Bulleted format pulls out information while paragraphs allow more to fit on a page

Front-Desk Cashier   Summer 2002
Microtel Inn & Suites ~ Hamilton, Michigan
- Handled complaints from customers and worked out solutions for both customer and company satisfaction
- Worked night audit and calculated the books for that specific night, then compared the numbers to previous year
- Greeted customers and assigned them to their rooms
- Collected cash and made change for customers
- Posted charges to their account when necessary
- Developed communications skills

COLLEGE ACTIVITIES

Sigma Phi Epsilon Fraternity   Fall 2002– Present
- New Recruitment Board
  Meet with other members to discuss events and make decisions on potential new members
- Brother Liaison
  Made calls to other members to inform them of important dates and meetings
- Brother Mentor
  Mentored new members and helped them through the first steps of being in the fraternity
- Community Service Hours–Promoted goodwill to the community with such activities as the Adopt-A-Highway Program, bowling with the elderly, Humane Society, and raising money for ALS (Lou Gehrig's Disease)

COMPUTER SKILLS

Integrate into profile after more work experience

Microsoft (Word, Works, Excel, PowerPoint, Access), MS-DOS

Word Count: 324

Angelo Rodriquez

Present Address: 600 E. 5th St., Holland, MI 89057   (316) 592-5280
Permanent Address: 3060 S. Holden St., Hamilton, MI 87057   (308) 769-9769
E-Mail Address: Arodriquez@hope.edu

Clearly and precisely points out top qualities

PROFILE

Developed excellent persuasive skills at internship and marketing assistant positions. Solid understanding of marketing concepts including cold calls, promotions, creative design, and selling. Demonstrate the ability to pay attention to detail at credit union and as front-desk manager. Professional demeanor exhibited at promotional events and sales calls. Computer skills in Microsoft Office (Word, Works, Excel, PowerPoint, Access), MS-DOS, and Microsoft Publisher.

EDUCATION

Bachelor of Science, Double Major: Business Management and Marketing   December 2005
Hope College, Holland, Michigan
Worked 15 hours a week while attending school full-time.

Variety of jobs show range of abilities and qualifications

EXPERIENCE

Teller   May 2005–Present
Northwest Credit Union ~ Holland, Michigan
Handle customers by depositing and withdrawing money from their accounts, transferring funds from one account to another, and responding to their requests through the drive-up window and over the phone. Handle loan payments and loan transfers. Work out solutions to customer problems to the satisfaction of the customer and company. Fine-tuned ability to pay attention to detail.

Marketing Intern   Summer 2005
CAP - Centers for Athletic Performance ~ Hamilton, Michigan
Completed a 40 hour training course to be qualified to educate and improve an athlete's performance through the use of advanced cutting-edge training. Made contacts with high school and college coaches to get CAP's name out and to promote the program, which resulted in new clients. Attended special events and camps to promote CAP. Tested athletes with cutting-edge equipment on and off location for CAP's database. Created flyers and banners for promotional purposes.

Marketing Assistant   August 2004–May 2005
Hope College Athletic Department ~ Holland, Michigan
Assisted the Athletic Marketing Director at Hope College with promotions, marketing, and public relations. Developed a relationship with local businesses in the area for promotional purposes and carried out the promotion at sporting events for the university. Responsibilities included half-time shows, music, special advertising announcements, and offers for the fans.

Front-Desk Manager   Summer 2002 & 2004
Microtel Inn & Suites ~ Hamilton, Michigan
Worked night audit and balanced the books for that specific night, then compared the numbers to the previous year to date. Used quick thinking and problem-solving skills to solve customer concerns. Developed communication skills by listening and interacting with customers on the phone and in person.

Construction Materials Delivery   Summer 2003
Rew Materials ~ Hamilton, Michigan
Worked 40 to 70 hours a week in the summer. Delivered sheetrock, insulation, and supplies to construction sites by truck. Maintained delivery log verifying material delivered and miles traveled. Lifted and carried heavy materials for deliveries. Developed ability to pay attention to detail.

COLLEGE ACTIVITIES

American Marketing Association   Fall 2004–Present

Minimizes this area after gaining more experience

Sigma Phi Epsilon Fraternity   Fall 2002–Present
- Junior Marshall
- New Recruitment Board
- Community Service Hours–Promoted goodwill to the community with such activities as bowling with the elderly, Humane Society, Adopt-A-Highway, and raising money for ALS

Word Count: 520

Caroline Morley

Current Address
1205 University Place #922
Columbia, MO 65201
(375) 814-6570

cmorley@yahoo.com

Permanent Address
942 West 20th
Centerville, MO 65640
(600) 562-3520

Objective:
    To obtain a marketing internship for this summer

Education:

University of Missouri – Columbia
Bachelor of Science in Business Administration – Marketing Concentration   GPA: 3.8/4.0
Anticipated Graduation: May 2006

Edith Cowan University – Perth, Australia   7/2004–12/2004

(callout: Missing impressive position titles)

(callout: Expand on overseas education experience)

Work Experience:

8/05–12/05   General Growth Properties   Columbia, MO
- Organized, administered, and maintained numerous mall events and programs, including launching the *Savings U* college campaign, charity and special group functions, as well as Thanksgiving Doorbuster and Christmas – *A Wonderful Night to Share* event (the largest and busiest mall events of the year).
- Supervised and assisted in day-to-day operations involved with running a modern shopping center

8/05-Present   University of Missouri Athletic Marketing Department   Columbia, MO
- Publicized University of Missouri Athletic events throughout the student body and community
- Conducted special promotions during various University of Missouri Athletic events

5/05-8/05   Show-Me State Games   Columbia, MO
- Oversaw and organized over 25,000 participants, volunteers, and staff from across the state of Missouri
- Negotiated with local restaurants and hotels to obtain donations for staff and volunteers during the events
- Drafted press releases for newspapers across the state and developed promotional material to increase local awareness

1/04–5/05   Missouri Student Federal Credit Union   Columbia, MO
Intern/Marketing Team
- Assisted customers with banking needs and performed internal banking activities and procedures
- Implemented new marketing strategies to broaden student awareness

(callout: Broaden work descriptions)

Activities:
University of Missouri Club Volleyball Team
AIESEC (International Internship Program) – Corporate Team
- Coordinated and conducted sales meetings with local businesses
Business Week 2004 Steering Committee – Marketing/Promotions Team
- Created theme used throughout entire Business Week
- Researched and compiled data from past Business Weeks, and utilized the findings to create promotions aimed to reach and inform the entire business school student body
Phi Beta Lambda Business Fraternity – Public Relations Committee
- Arranged for informative, relevant guest speakers to appear at each meeting
Residence Hall Government – Recreational Sports Chair
Humane Society Volunteer
United Way Day of Caring – Food Drive Volunteer
University of Missouri Study Abroad Office Volunteer

Honors:
- Dean's List: 5 consecutive semesters
- Boeing Scholar
- University of Missouri Excellence Scholarship
- Honors College Member

Word Count: 413

Caroline Morley

1205 University Place #922 ~ Columbia, MO 65201 ~ (375) 814-6570 ~ cmorley@yahoo.com

---

OBJECTIVE   To obtain a marketing internship at Radio Shack

EDUCATION

Bachelor of Science Degree in Business Administration – Marketing Concentration   May 2006
University of Missouri – Columbia, Missouri   GPA: 3.8/4.0

Study Abroad (Edith Cowan University, Perth, Australia) – Fall 2004

Select Honors: Dean's List – (5 consecutive semesters), University of Missouri Excellence Scholarship,
Honors College Member, Boeing Scholar

WORK EXPERIENCE

Office/Event Assistant ~ **University of Missouri Athletic Marketing Department** ~ **Columbia, Missouri**   **Aug. 2005 – Present**
- Publicize University of Missouri athletic events throughout the student body and community using heavy distribution of media materials, special events/functions (MIZZOU Madness/men's basketball scrimmage), and numerous targeted programs aimed at specific demographic segments (Truman Club, Spirit Passes). Conduct special promotions during University of Missouri athletic events and direct half-time activities.

Prodigy Intern ~ **General Growth Properties** ~ **Columbia, Missouri**   **Aug. 2005 – Dec. 2005**
- Organized, administered, and maintained numerous mall events and campaigns, including launching the Savings U college campaign, charity and special group functions, Tiger Pep Rally, and Thanksgiving Doorbuster and Christmas event (the largest and busiest mall events of the year). Supervised and assisted in day-to-day operations involved with running a modern shopping center by working with leasing, finance, and operations departments and monitoring all in-mall signage, mall Web page, and general marketing/merchant correspondence.

Administrative Assistant/Fund-Raising Coordinator ~ **Show-Me State Games** ~ **Columbia, Missouri**   **Summer 2005**
- Oversaw and organized over 25,000 participants, volunteers, and staff from across the state of Missouri. Negotiated with local restaurants and hotels to obtain donations for over 100 rooms and 2,500 meals for staff, volunteers, and opening ceremonies keynote speaker George Foreman. Drafted press releases and compiled information on "Athletes of Interest" to distribute to television stations and newspapers across the state of Missouri.

Intern/Marketing Team ~ **Missouri Student Federal Credit Union** ~ **Columbia, Missouri**   **Jan. 2004 – May 2005**
- Communicated with customers to make banking transactions effective. Implemented new marketing strategies to broaden student awareness such as giveaways, strategically placed advertisements (University newspaper, table tents in dining halls, logo placement on Business Week fund-raising T-shirts), and special offers (spring-break loans, free gift with new account, Summer Welcome coupons).

LEADERSHIP ACTIVITIES

- University of Missouri Club Volleyball Team – Aug. 2003 – May 2005
- Business Week 2004 Steering Committee – Marketing/Promotions Team
  - Created "There's no Business like MO Business" theme used throughout entire Business Week
  - Researched and compiled data from past Business Weeks, and utilized the findings to create promotions aimed to reach and inform the entire business school student body; as a result observed a 300% increase in both group and individual participation during the events activities
- *AIESEC (International Internship Program) – Corporate Team*
  - Coordinated and conducted sales meetings with local businesses to create partnerships and enable skilled individuals from over 85 countries to participate in traineeship positions in Columbia and surrounding areas
- Phi Beta Lambda Business Fraternity – Public Relations Committee
- Residence Hall Government – Recreational Sports Chair
- Community Service Activities - Humane Society and United Way Day of Caring Food Drive
- University of Missouri Study Abroad Office Volunteer (10 hours per week)

PORTFOLIO AVAILABLE

Word Count: 521

Teri Carlson

339 South Main
Stanford, CA 94468
(819)-123-5597
E-mail: tcarlson@stanford.edu

2324 Diamond Ave.
Seattle, Washington 65657
(641)-585-3392
tcarlson@hotmail.com

Right margin is too large

Objective
Fashion Merchandising Management Internship

Education
Bachelor of Science in Merchandising of Textiles, Apparel, and Furnishings   GPA 3.88/4.0
Minor: Business
Stanford University   Graduation Date, Spring 2006

Relevant Courses
Creating Aesthetic Environments, Apparel Selection, Textile and Apparel Industries, Visual Merchandising, Textiles, Merchandising/Retail Math, Home Equipment, Computer-Aided Design

Needs stronger section headings

Computer Skills
Microsoft Word, Excel, Access, PowerPoint, Internet Explorer, CAD

Activities/Honors
Phi Eta Sigma National Honor Society
Alpha Chi National College Honor Society
Kappa Omicron Nu National Honor Society
•   Publicity Chair 2004 – 2005, Medallion Chair 2005 – 2006
•   Family and Consumer Sciences Week Planning Committee–Public Relations 2004 – 2005
•   Merchandising of Textiles, Apparel, and Furnishings Ambassador 2005 – 2006

Space is wasted and section is too high on the résumé

Work Experience
Technical Writer, Quality Engineering Department
Energizer Battery Co.   Stanford, CA   June 2004 – present
•   Create technical training documents for quality control testing by discussing processes with employees and entering the step-by-step process into a Structured On the Job Training (SOJT) document template
•   Organize quality control data into Excel and create graphs and charts for comparison
•   Time-management and teamwork skills enhanced through project responsibility and leadership

Bank Teller
Citizens Bank   Seattle, WA   July 2003 – May 2004
•   Assisted customers with transactions, such as cash, personal and cashier's checks, and savings bonds
•   Handled $100's of dollars a day; worked with the public serving 100 – 150 customers a day
•   Worked with copy machine, fax machine, teller machine, and money counter; filed documents, answered phones, and took messages

Leave off unrelated positions if more relevant work experience is available

Waitress
Ice House Restaurant and Lounge   Seattle, WA   Summer 2003
•   Greeted and seated customers; took food and drink orders
•   Worked with customers, cooks, and bartenders in a variety of atmospheres including the bar, casual eating area, and formal dining area
•   Assisted customers with tickets and money

Cash Register Attendant and Cook
Farmers Mutual Town & Country   Seattle, WA   Summer 2002
•   Opened and closed the store
•   Maintained personal cash drawer and the money that passed through it daily
•   Worked with the public serving approximately 150 – 250 people a day, prepared food for two meals a day in a commercial oven
•   Stocked shelves and kept store clean and organized

Word Count: 372

Teri Carlson

339 South Main
Stanford, CA 94468
(819) 123-5597
tcarlson@stanford.edu

Just use one address so not seen as a new graduate

OBJECTIVE

Fashion Merchandising Management Internship for Dillards

EDUCATION

Bachelor of Science Degree in Merchandising of Textiles, Apparel, and Furnishings, Minor: Business   April 2006
Stanford University, Stanford, California   GPA: 3.88/4.0
Work 15–20 hours per week while attending school full-time

Courses Related to Merchandising

Apparel Selection	Textiles	Creating Aesthetic Environments
Textile and Apparel Industries	Visual Merchandising	Home Equipment
Analysis of Sewn Products	Merchandising/Retail Math	Computer-Aided Design (CAD)

INTERNSHIP EXPERIENCE

Sales Associate, Intern

Lerner New York & Co.   Seattle, Washington   Summer 2005
- Greeted and assisted customers with purchase decisions, created visually pleasing ensembles, and set up wall and window displays daily
- Practiced sales strategies by notifying customers of current sales and promotional deals taking place
- Worked with a team of up to three Sales Associates and Managers to create an atmosphere in which customers felt comfortable in order to maximize sales
- Enhanced understanding of product construction, type, and design
- Received an offer for further employment over the Thanksgiving and Christmas holiday seasons

WORK EXPERIENCE

Technical Writer, Quality Engineering Department

Energizer Battery Co.   Stanford, California   June 2004–present
- Create training documents for quality control testing procedures after discussing processes with employees
- Enter the step-by-step process into a Structured On the Job Training (SOJT) document template
- Organize quality control data into Excel and create graphs and charts for comparison
- Time-management and teamwork skills enhanced through project responsibility and leadership

Bank Teller

Citizens Bank   Seattle, Washington   July 2003–May 2004
- Assisted customers with banking transactions
- Handled thousands of dollars each shift, worked with the public serving 100–150 customers daily
- Worked with copy, fax, teller machines, and money counter; filed documents, answered phones, and took messages

ACTIVITIES/HONORS

- Kappa Omicron Nu National Honor Society Publicity Chair 2004–2005, Medallion Chair 2005, 2006, Family and Consumer Sciences Week Planning Committee-Public Relations 2004–2005

- Merchandising of Textiles, Apparel, and Furnishings Ambassador 2005–2006

- Phi Eta Sigma National Honor Society

- Alpha Chi National College Honor Society

COMPUTER SKILLS

Microsoft (Word, Excel, Access, PowerPoint), Internet Explorer, computer-aided design (CAD)

Word Count: 379

Lynette Johnson

305 Crysler Court
Kansas City, Missouri 64233
(816) 356-8609

611 N. Country Club Dr. #2
Emporia, Kansas 68455
(785) 562-8204

Ljohnson@hotmail.com

OBJECTIVE

To obtain a challenging internship in my field

Unfocused

HIGHLIGHTS OF SKILLS

- Proficient in Microsoft Office, QuarkXPress, PhotoShop, PowerPoint, and Ad Creator

- Enjoy working with people

Need 3–6 items in profile or summary section

EDUCATION

Bachelor of Science in Speech Communications and Public Relations   December 2007
Emporia State University, Emporia, Kansas, GPA 3.2
Lambda Pi Eta Communications Honor Society
Member of Public Relations Student Society of America

PROFESSIONAL EXPERIENCE

Member Service Representative ~ RLSC Credit Union ~ Raytown, MO   2/04–Present
- Assist members with new accounts and daily transactions
- Organize insurance and perform data entry

Event Coordinator/Caterer ~ Joe's Barn Catering ~ Raytown, MO   10/01–8/05
- Organized and booked catering events for groups of 20–300
- Provided information regarding menu items, prices, and setup
- Developed list of supplies, scheduled servers, and coordinated setup
- Trained and advised co-workers to provide excellent customer service
- Prepared and served clients at catering events

Jobs focus only on duties, needs accomplishments

Public Relations Chair ~ Alpha Sigma Alpha ~ Emporia, KS   2/05–8/05
- Corresponded with community newspapers for sorority events
- Planned and aided in organization of Centennial Celebration
- Created awareness of sorority events designing fliers
- Served on Panhellenic Council

Sales Associate ~ Student Body ~ Emporia, KS   2/04–6/04
- Aided customers purchasing sportswear, company attire, and various memorabilia
- Provided guidance to customers special ordering products

Word Count: 242

Lynette Johnson

Permanent: 305 Crysler Court
Kansas City, MO 64233
(816) 356-8609

Current: 611 N. Country Club Dr. #2
Emporia, KS 68455
(785) 562-8204

Ljohnson@hotmail.com

OBJECTIVE

To obtain a challenging internship with Starlight Theatre in the Marketing or Event Coordination area

HIGHLIGHTS OF SKILLS

- Experience with teamwork and creativity
- Adept problem-solving skills
- Proficient in Microsoft Office, QuarkXpress, PhotoShop, PowerPoint, and Ad Creator

- Embrace change and innovation
- Experience in retail and service
- Self-motivated student and worker

EDUCATION

Bachelor of Science in Speech Communications and Public Relations   December 2007
Emporia State University, Emporia, Kansas   Overall 3.2   Major 3.6
Lambda Pi Eta Communications Honor Society–top 1/3 of students
Member of Public Relations Student Society of America

PROFESSIONAL EXPERIENCE

Member Service Representative ~ RLSC Credit Union ~ Raytown, Missouri   Feb. 2004–Present
- Assist members with new accounts and daily transactions.
- Foster positive customer relations between members and staff.
- Organize insurance forms and perform data entry.
- Position requires extreme attention to detail and initiative to improve efficiency.

Event Coordinator/Caterer ~ Joe's Barn Catering ~ Raytown, Missouri   Oct. 2001–Aug. 2005
- Organized and booked catering events for groups of 20–300.
- Provided information regarding menu items, prices, and setup.
- Developed list of supplies, scheduled servers, and coordinated setup.
- Trained and advised co-workers to provide excellent customer service.
- Prepared and served clients at catering events.
- Fine-tuned ability to solve problems in a situation that required an immediate solution.

Public Relations Chair ~ Alpha Sigma Alpha ~ Emporia, Kansas   Feb. 2005–Aug. 2005
- Corresponded with community newspapers for sorority events.
- Planned and aided in organization of Centennial Celebration.
  - Attended national conference in Virginia to discuss individual chapter planning.
  - Planned and coordinated weekend celebration for 40 members and 80 alumni.
  - Delegated work and followed up to ensure timely completion of duties.
- Created awareness of sorority events designing fliers.
- Served on Panhellenic Council.

Sales Associate ~ Student Body ~ Emporia, Kansas   Feb. 2004–June 2004
- Aided customers purchasing sportswear, company attire, and memorabilia.
- Provided guidance to customers special ordering products.
- Organized product displays and maintained a neat store appearance.

Word Count: 364

■ SPECIAL SITUATIONS

Cindy Haddok—High School to College
Cindy's first attempt resulted in 32 words on a second page. A simple format change such as using two columns for her activities freed up the space she needed to fit her information on one page.

Dai-Hua Tung—Early in Your College Career
Dai-Hua needed to include high school activities to fill up his page; this is a reasonable approach for college sophomores. When creativity is a key element of a field like horticulture, using a visual element such as professional clip art can help an applicant stand out in the pile of résumés.

Tyler Kenkel—Focus on Sports
Tyler needed to camouflage his flaws (low GPA) and draw attention to his best feature (a successful collegiate basketball career).

Darbi Thurman—Nontraditional Student
Darbi's résumé needed updating to allow her soon-to-be-completed AAS degree to be added. While taking her employment strategies course, she realized just how sorry her previous version looked. Darbi added accessories (a bulleted accomplishment at the end of each position description) to show that she has excelled in all of her positions. Education follows work experience for nontraditional students.

Keenan Joiner—Functional (Two-Page Version)
Keenan uses a functional format to tailor his skills to the employer's needs. He pulled skills and accomplishments from his diverse work history to clearly show LMP how his unique experience would fit their needs. This résumé allowed him to move from a laborer position to a management role.

CINDY HADDOCK

2000 Spaulding Street
Omaha, NE 68104
Phone: (402) 453-7200
E-mail: Chaddock@cox.net

OBJECTIVE

To obtain employment in the business department at Northwest Missouri State University through the freshman work-study program.

EDUCATION

High School Diploma: May 2006   GPA: 3.8   Class Rank: 7 of 257
Benson High School   Omaha, NE
Possess excellent computer skills: Microsoft (Word, Excel, PowerPoint), Internet Explorer

ACTIVITIES

Retain high school information until after first year of college

- National Honor Society
  - Habitat for Humanity
  - Shopping for Visually Impaired
  - Relay for Life
  - Drug Awareness Program
- Cheerleading (4 years)
  - Junior Varsity Captain
- Student Council
  - Council Relations Coordinator
  - Homecoming Committee
  - Prom Committee
  - District Eight Conventions
- Academy of Finance
- Physics Club

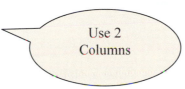

Use 2 Columns

EMPLOYMENT

<u>Server</u>, Danny's Bar and Grill ~ Omaha, NE   2/2004 – 8/2006
- Provide customer service by responding to customer requests in an accurate, friendly, and timely manner in neighborhood restaurant.
- Clear and clean tables to maintain a tidy work area.
- Work 15 – 20 hours a week while remaining active in school.

<u>Property Management Assistant</u>, Boynton Rentals ~ Omaha, NE   5/01 – present
- Show prospective clients rental units and explain terms of contracts.
- Solve tenant problems dealing with lockouts, noise complaints, plumbing, electrical issues.
- Clean and paint rental units under short time frames to allow for quick turnaround of units.
- Collect and record rent and deposits.

<u>Child Care,</u> Susan Keyser   5/02 – 2/04
- Tended to 3 children ages infant to 8 years old.

Next page had awards with only 4 lines. She needed to get it all on one page

Word Count: 245

CINDY HADDOCK

2000 Spaulding Street
Omaha, NE 68104
Phone: (402) 453-7200
E-mail: Chaddock@cox.net

OBJECTIVE

To obtain employment in the business department at the University of Nebraska through the freshman work-study program.

EDUCATION

High School Diploma: May 2006   GPA: 3.8   Class Rank: 7 of 257
Benson High School,   Omaha, Nebraska
Possess excellent computer skills: Microsoft (Word, Excel, PowerPoint), Internet Explorer

ACTIVITIES

- National Honor Society
  o Habitat for Humanity
  o Shopping for Visually Impaired
  o Relay for Life
  o Drug Awareness Program
- Cheerleading (4 years)
  o Junior Varsity Captain

- Student Council
  o Council Relations Coordinator
  o Homecoming Committee
  o Prom Committee
  o District Eight Conventions
- Academy of Finance
- Physics Club

EMPLOYMENT

Server, Danny's Bar and Grill ~ Omaha, Nebraska   Feb. 2004 – Aug. 2006
- Provide customer service by responding to customer requests in an accurate, friendly, and timely manner in neighborhood restaurant.
- Clear and clean tables to maintain a tidy work area.
- Work 15 – 20 hours a week while remaining active in school.

Property Management Assistant, Boynton Rentals ~ Omaha, Nebraska   May 2001 – present
- Show prospective clients rental units and explain terms of contracts.
- Solve tenant problems dealing with lockouts, noise complaints, plumbing and electrical issues.
- Clean and paint rental units under short time frames to allow for quick turnaround of units.
- Collect and record rent and deposits.

Child Care, Susan Keyser   May 2002 – Feb. 2004
- Tended to 3 children ages infant to 8 years old.

AWARDS RECEIVED

- Three-year recipient of Academic Letter Award (Requires GPA of 3.75 or higher)
- Honor Roll (8 semesters)
- Most Spirited/Outstanding PomPom Performer (Cheerleading)
- Math Student of the Month (3 times)

Word Count: 277

Dai-Hua Tung
3021 Springfield, MO 65801

(417) 601-8897
Dtung@hotmail.net

OBJECTIVE

Subtle but effective use of clip art

To obtain a Summer 2006 internship at Hometown Landscape and Lawn Service in Silver Spring, Maryland.

EDUCATION

Bachelor of Science Degree with a Major in Horticulture, emphasis Landscape Design   May 2008
Minor in General Business
Southwest Missouri State University ~ Springfield, Missouri   GPA: 3.35/4.0
   Relevant coursework to be completed by Summer 2006:
   - Woody Landscape Plants
   - Turfgrass Management
   - Plant Science
   - Plant Diseases

WORK EXPERIENCE

Production Worker ~ Sunshine Electronic Display ~ Joplin, Missouri   June 2002 – January 2006
                                                                              (during school breaks)

   - Mentored new hires and fellow employees
   - Constructed wooden crates for shipment of signs
   - Customized raw metal for sign construction
   - Built control boxes for mechanized signs
   - Vinyled sign displays

Laborer ~ Garden/Lawn Service ~ Joplin, Missouri   May 2002 – June 2002

   - Worked labor projects for a 5-acre yard
   - Planted and maintained vegetables in a half-acre garden
   - Built bean fences and cleared brush
   - Work was largely unsupervised

HONORS AND ACHIEVEMENTS

High School:
   - All State Basketball
   - All State Track
   - All Conference Football
   - Perfect Attendance
   - Principal's Honor Roll (7/8 Semesters)

College:
   - SMSU Regents Scholarship
   - Clarksdale Lions Club Scholarship
   - National Honor Society Scholarship
   - SMSU Honor Roll (all semesters)

LEADERSHIP ACTIVITIES

   - Captain of high school basketball, football, and track team
   - High school senior class president and representative
   - Vice president of National Honor Society in high school
   - College Intramural participant in football and basketball

Only appropriate to use high school if just a sophomore

COMPUTER SKILLS

   - Microsoft (Windows, PowerPoint, Works, Word, Excel, and Paint)
   - Internet search engines

Word Count: 259

Tyler Kenkel

Focus is on athletics vs. academics

614 East First ~ Maryville, MO ~ (660) 582-4412 ~ E-mail~ TKenkel@hotmail.com

PROFILE

- Exceptional ability to motivate teammates to work toward goals and achieve their full athletic potential.
- Hardworking, disciplined, and dependable individual that projects self-confidence, authority, and enthusiasm.
- Demonstrate leadership on and off the court by leading a life that serves as a positive role model to teammates and local community.
- Comfortable speaking before small and large community groups on a variety of topics relating to values, confidence, leadership, and teamwork.

EDUCATION

Bachelor of Science with a Double Major: Business Management and Marketing   **June 2004**
Northwest Missouri State University ~ Maryville, Missouri
- Finance education with athletic scholarship and summer work.
- Demonstrate excellent time-management skills balancing practices, games, and full load of classes while maintaining commitment to both basketball and academics.

Select Athletic Accomplishments
- First player in Northwest history to achieve over 100 wins in a career.
- Skilled point guard who led team to win conference and South central regional tournament championships in 2001–2002 and 2003–2004.
- Only Division II player nominated for Bob Cousey Award.
- Most Valuable Player of the MIAA, MIAA Defensive Player of the Year 2003 and 2004.

VOLUNTEER COACHING EXPERIENCE

Northwest Missouri State University ~ Maryville, Missouri
Basketball Camps   **Summers 2000–Present**
- Assisted men's basketball program in offering camps for players ages 7–18 developing fundamental skills. Encourage becoming a complete player and emphasize team play.
- Utilize exceptional oral communication skills to instruct and motivate players while enhancing their self-esteem.

PROFESSIONAL WORK EXPERIENCE

Wal-Mart Superstore ~ Maryville, Missouri
Bakery Department Coordinator   **Summer 2002**
- Used creativity to organize and rebuild daily product stands.
- Work was largely unsupervised requiring initiative and the ability to pay attention to detail.

K.C. Royals Stadium Club ~ Kansas City, Missouri
Suite Supervisor   **Summer 2000 and 2001**
- Provided services to a wide variety of customers renting out suites at the Royals stadium.
- Supervised groups of 6 to ensure excellent customer service was being provided.
- Performed with one of the most profitable teams in the stadium (consistently in top 10%).

Kansas City Missouri School District ~ Kansas City, Missouri
Student Mentor/Teaching Assistant   **Summer 1999**
- Taught, organized lessons, and facilitated classes with over 25 students.
- Skilled at motivating students to make personal advances that resulted in increased self-motivation and individual expectations of the students.
- Participated in Parent-Teacher Conferences and one-on-one parental meetings.

Word Count: 412

Darbi S. Thurman

242 State Hwy. E
Ravenwood, MO 64479
(660) 937-3600

Bullets too far away from text.

Relevant Experience

- Perform typing and word processing for management team.
- Operate copy machine, fax machine, 10-key adding machine, various computer printers.
- Responsible for typing and maintaining purchase orders.
- Answer and redirect incoming telephone calls.
- Order and maintain appropriate levels of office supplies.
- Maintain petty cash ($400.00). Notarize legal documents.
- Enroll employees in company benefit programs and answer questions (health, dental, life, 401(k), pension, workers' compensation).
- Facilitate and handle workers' compensation in absence of Human Resource Manager; correspond with and telephone physicians' offices, hospitals, and employees regarding health insurance and workers' compensation claims.
- Enter new employee information and maintain employee records in ABRA (human resource computer system) and create reports as necessary.
- Assisted in employee selection process by screening applicants, scheduling interviews co-interviewing applicants and performed employee orientation.
- Set up preemployment physical examinations and drug screens.
- Maintain personnel and medical files.
- Answer questions regarding job openings and process incoming applications.
- Solicited and compiled employee safety suggestions. Served on Ergonomics Committee.
- Organized and directed Industry/Education Day - October '97.
- Manage employee purchases of company products, safety shoes, and glasses.

Employment History

Laclede Chain Mfg. Company	Maryville, MO	1985 – Present
Cottonwood Manor	Yukon, OK	1983 – 1985

Can leave off long-ago, unrelated positions

Computer Skills

Windows 95/XP	Microsoft Works 4.0	ABRA 2000
Windows 3.1	Mainframe System	PrintShop

Education

AAS Degree in Business Management	May 2005
North Central Missouri College, Trenton, Missouri	Overall GPA 4.0

Human Resource Management Course, Northwest Missouri State University,
Maryville, Missouri - Fall of 1997 (received an A)

Certified Nurses Aide Course, Pikes Peak Community College,
Colorado Springs, Colorado - 1980 (4.0 GPA)

Seminars: Motivational, Leading Through Chaos, Conflict and Confrontation

Diploma, Florence High School, Florence, Colorado - 1980

Reference Available Upon Request

Darbi Thurman

242 State Hwy. E
Ravenwood, MO 64479

660-937-3600
darbithurm@asde.net

OBJECTIVE

Management Position with LMP Steel & Wire

PROFESSIONAL EXPERIENCE

<u>Laclede Chain Manufacturing Co.</u>, Maryville, Missouri

KEY

ATTRIBUTES:

Accounting Assistant – Promotion   2004 – present

Cost new products for sales managers, enter new product numbers and information in mainframe computer system, assist office manager with day-to-day accounting issues, compile data daily from production areas and produce reports, continue to fulfill administrative assistant duties.

Accurate

Detail oriented

Administrative Assistant – Promotion   2000 – 2004

Provided administrative/secretarial support for a number of departments, answered 5-line phone system, and directed visitors to appropriate personnel. Established, maintained, and updated files, databases, records, and/or other documents, requisitioned and ordered office supplies as needed. Revised, distributed, and controlled ISO documents as required by the company's internal quality system. Maintained petty cash ($500.00) and notarized legal documents, and continued to fulfill many of previous positions.
> ➢ *Instrumental in helping secure ISO accreditation in 2004.*

Dependable

Tenacious

Secretary/Human Resource Assistant   1993 – 2000

Enrolled employees in company benefit programs and answer questions (health, dental, life, 401(k), pension, workers' compensation), assisted in employee selection process by screening applicants, scheduling interviews, co-interviewing applicants and performed employee orientation, set up preemployment physical examinations and drug screens, maintained personnel and medical files, solicited and compiled employee safety suggestions, and performed typing and word processing for management team.
> ➢ *Organized highly successful industry education day.*

PERSONABLE

Quick
Learner

Laborer   1989 – 1993

Assembled tire chains with a team of 5. Frequently volunteered for overtime. Always willing to work in other departments when needed.
> ➢ *Chosen three times as Employee of the Quarter.*

Professional

DILIGENT

EDUCATION

AAS Degree in Business Management   May 2006
North Central Missouri College, Trenton, Missouri   Overall GPA 4.0
> ➢ Work full-time while taking full-time courses
> ➢ President's List all semesters

PERCEPTIVE

Flexible

COMPUTER SKILLS

Operating Systems	**Creative Software**	**Financial/Specialized**
Microsoft Windows '98, XP	Microsoft Word	Microsoft Excel
Business Mainframe	Microsoft Publisher	Microsoft Access
	Microsoft PowerPoint	Abra Suite

ENERGETIC

Respectable

ORGANIZATIONS & ACTIVITIES

Beta Sigma Phi Sorority/Omega Phi Chapter, Ravenwood, Missouri   1998 – present

Keenan Joiner

923 S. Main Street, St. Joseph, MO 64501   816-937-1234   keenan.joiner@us.army.mil

OBJECTIVE

To assist LMP Steel implement a first-class health and safety program.

PROFILE

- Effectively develops individual, departmental, and organizational goals to obtain objective.
- Exercises sound judgment on behalf of others; can be open minded when forming opinions.
- Takes prompt measures to prevent performance and behavior problems from becoming irreversible.
- Uses systematic methods to accomplish more in less time.

RELATED EXPERIENCE

Safety – 17 years' experience relating to health and safety programs.
- Solid understanding of production process and dangers of industrial environments.
- Trained in lockout/tagout and confined safety procedures.
- Completed rigorous fire prevention and fire fighting procedures.
- Basic understanding of OSHA rules and regulations.

Health – well versed in providing emergency medical care in a variety of settings.
- Established and maintained a medical clinic in Kuwait and Qatar that treated up to 38,000 – 40,000 troops over a six-month period with a team of 35.
- Served as a EMT for seven and a half years; earned a reputation as a empathetic care provider.
- Trained in first aid, CPR, blood borne pathogens, basic trauma life support. Able to quickly assess the nature and extent of an injury and make lifesaving decisions.

Training – experience training in areas involving health care, safety, defensive tactics, and enhancing morale and ethics in the workplace.
- Completed a course on designing and implementing successful training programs.
- Used clear and sensible instructions to protect soldiers from injury and equipment from damage.
- Used motivation skills for both individuals and groups to learn how the military philosophy benefits the platoon's readiness.

Leadership – exceptional skills developed through courses and hands-on experience, down-to-earth communication style that works well with production workers, supervisors, and employees from diverse cultures.
- Effectively establishes work priorities and organizes work schedules for 5 – 7 subordinates.
- Assigned duties and instructed subordinates in work techniques and procedures.
- Counseled personnel and prepared evaluation reports.
- Continually searches for ways to improve section.
- Uses common sense in problem solving to make logical decisions.

Keenan Joiner – Résumé Page 2

It is still important to show your jobs and their dates

EDUCATION & RELEVANT TRAINING

Employee Performance Planning & Appraisal (2004)
Supervising a Harassment Free Workplace (2004)
Conflict Management (2003)
Basic Supervision Class (2003)
Train the Trainer (2003)

Interviewing and Staff Selection Tools (2003)
US Army Combat Life Savers Course (2002)
United States Army Medical Training Course (2002)
Vocational School EMT Course (1991)

WORK HISTORY

Staff Sergeant	Missouri Army National Guard ~ St. Joseph, Missouri	Jan. 1986 – Present
Laborer	Kawasaki Motors ~ Maryville, Missouri	Sept. 2003 – Present
Medic - Active Duty	Army National Guard ~ Kuwait	May 2002 – Sept. 2003
Corrections Supervisor	Missouri Department of Corrections ~ Maryville, Missouri	Feb. 2002 – Dec. 2002
Airport Security - Active Duty	Army National Guard ~ Kansas City, Missouri	Nov. 2001 – May 2002
Deputy Sheriff	Nodaway County Sheriff Department ~ Maryville, Missouri	Oct. 1997 – Jan. 1998
EMT	Nodaway County Ambulance ~ Maryville, Missouri	June 1991 – Oct. 1998

REFERENCES

Lt. Anthony Groumoutis
Training Officer/E-squad Commander
Maryville Treatment Center
Maryville, MO 64468
660-814-6535

Lt. Kyle Scott
Physician's Assistant
Army National Guard
Maryville, MO 64468
660-814-5656

SFC Brian Espey
Readiness Officer
Army National Guard
St. Joseph, MO 54501
816-274-8276

Mr. Alex Snow
Former Ambulance Director
Nodaway County Ambulance District
Maryville, MO 64468
660-582-8488

SFC William Payne
Readiness Officer
Army National Guard
St. Joseph, MO 54501
816-274-8276

Ms. Brea Yates
Human Resource Manager
Kawasaki Motors
Maryville, MO 64468
660-562-8484

Word Count: 519

Functional layouts work well when trying to change professions or incorporate military experience into your résumé

Electronic Résumé Guidelines

<u>How many versions of my résumé do I need? I keep hearing about scannable and electronic résumés, but I don't have one.</u>

While traditional "paper copy" résumés are still used at many organizations, electronic résumés are also a necessity. The most important thing to remember is to check with a prospective employer to determine their preferred method of receiving your cover letter and résumé. While there is extra work involved, scannable and electronic résumés easily are created by making a few quick changes to your traditional résumé. Although some sources recommend adding a keywords section to your electronic version, you shouldn't need to adjust your résumé if you followed the earlier directions regarding incorporating keywords into your "traditional" résumé.

A brief definition of the most common résumé formats is included along with directions for converting your traditional résumé. These directions were written with the most novice computer user in mind.

TRADITIONAL

Paper Copy. Attractively formatted with a word processing program, the most popular is Microsoft Word although some people prefer Corel WordPerfect. It can be mailed, faxed, or hand delivered with a cover letter to the prospective employer.

ELECTRONIC

Hard Copy (on paper). Actually becomes an electronic résumé after it is scanned into an applicant tracking system such as Resumix using optical character recognition (OCR) software and then placing it into a keyword-searchable database.

Attachment. Electronic file saved in your word processing format and sent as an attachment. Maintains most of its formatting, but it can vary from computer to computer; can only be opened with appropriate software; employers are often afraid to open these because they may contain viruses. Many employers prefer that your résumé be submitted in this format, but it is always a good idea to check prior to submitting it this way.

TXT. An electronic file of your scannable résumé can be sent as a ASCII text-based .txt file; it will lose most of the traditional formatting, but carries little chance of having viruses and is compatible with all computer programs.

PDF. Electronic file saved as a PDF (Portable Document File) and sent as an attachment maintains its formatting. The file can be viewed on all platforms (sometimes you have to download free reader software) and is free from virus concerns; it does, however, require special software to create a .pdf file and the files you send will be quite large.

RTF. Electronic file saved as .rtf (Rich Text Format) and sent as an attachment; loses advanced formatting but can be opened with all word processing programs and is less susceptible to viruses.

■ CREATE A SCANNER- AND E-MAIL-READY RÉSUMÉ

1. Open the résumé that you have previously created in Microsoft Word.

2. Click File and Save As to save a copy of the file. Give it a different name from the original (i.e., *your_full_name_electronicresume.doc*). Using your full name in the file will make it easier for an employer to identify. Employers receive many résumés and a name "Resume.doc" is too generic.

3. You will now make modifications to the **version** you have just created.

4. The first change to make is to change all of the titles to all caps. (Many of you will already have your section headings capitalized.) To do this, simply highlight each title with the mouse and press and hold the following keys on the keyboard: Control (Ctrl) → Shift → A. It is important to note that you will have to make this change to each section heading/title individually.

5. Once you have finished changing the titles, press the following keys on the keyboard: Control (Ctrl) → A. This will highlight the entire document. If you have used a two- or three-column layout for any part of your project, while everything is highlighted click the column button on the toolbar and click in the space to the far left of that menu to put everything in one column.

6. In the left-hand top corner of the screen, directly to the left of font, there is a drop-down box. Click the arrow to drop the box down and click Clear Formatting or if you have an older version of Windows, you may need to select Normal.

7. Your résumé will now look very plain, as is desired. If you used text boxes for the titles, you may still need to delete them.

8. You may also have to make some changes so that information that was previously tabbed is now separated with a comma. If you haven't used periods with your position descriptions, you should now add them. Changing the margins (which automatically happened when you chose the Clear Formatting or Plain or Normal function) may have displaced dates, and so forth. It is OK if a date is on the line after your degree, employment, or education data. You may need to add commas to separate items.

9. Next, you only need to leave one blank line between each section, so delete any extra lines.

10. Although some sources say it is appropriate to underline on a scannable résumé, it is safest not to since j, p, q, g, and y can often touch an underline (jpqgy.) Add a space around dashes or hyphens so that none of the characters are touching one another (8-8). It is best to print the résumé to see if the letters are touching each other because they sometimes appear to touch on the screen but not after you have printed them.

11. On the left margin stack your name, address, each phone number, and e-mail addresses underneath the name. Each item will have its own line. Make sure you

have a space before and after the dash used in your phone number so that numbers aren't touching.

12. If any bullets are left, you want to take them out and replace them with asterisks or dashes so that they aren't interpreted as a letter like a hollow "o" bullet would be. Leave one space after each asterisk. Spell out any percent signs or ampersands because they may not scan properly.

13. Save the file. This is your Electronic Résumé rough draft.

14. You are almost done with your printable, scannable résumé. Most likely it will be over two pages, so you'll need to type "your name – page 2" on the second page. Next, go to File and Save As to save it again with a file name that identifies it as your printable, scannable version (i.e., *your_full_name_scannable_to_printresume.doc*).

15. Print the scannable version of your résumé on high-quality white paper using a high-quality laser printer. Mail your résumé in a flat 9 × 12 inch envelope without folding or stapling it. Use a paperclip on the top right corner (where there is no print) to keep your documents together. If using this option, you might also include a copy of your attractively formatted "traditional" résumé and your cover letter. Experts caution against faxing a résumé that will be scanned. Instead, offer to send it through express mail.

The next step will vary depending on the way your electronic résumé will be submitted. Simply look for the title in bold that fits your needs.

E-mailing in the body of an e-mail (not attaching):

Reopen the file you saved as *your_full_name_electronicresume.doc* in step 13.

1. Click on File and Save As. In the box that comes up, click the drop box next to Save as type and scroll down to Plain Text (.txt) Change the name of the file to note it is for sending within e-mail messages (i.e. *your_full_name_email_resume.txt*). Save your file in this format. In the box that opens now, choose the Windows (Default) radio button, check Insert line breaks, and then click OK.

2. Close the Word file and open the file saved in the .txt format (i.e., *your_full_name_email_resume.txt*). You will need to change the Save as type: from *.doc to *.txt.

3. Go to the end of your document and retype your contact information at the very end. Doing this will allow an employer to print the scannable résumé with your contact information on a second page as well as at the beginning of your document.

4. Click File and Save. You will now copy and paste the text into the body of your e-mail.

5. Press and hold Control (Ctrl) → A to highlight the entire document.

6. Press and hold Control (Ctrl) → C to copy all of the text to the computer's clipboard.

7. Click into the body of the e-mail you will be sending and press Control (Ctrl) → V to paste the text into the body of the e-mail. Check the body of your e-mail to see that the document looks the way you want it to. The examples below show what a difference appropriate wrapping can make within your message.

```
Proficient in Microsoft Office (Word, Excel, PowerPoint, Access), POS, Adobe
Reader, Internet
Explorer, and WordPerfect. Completed a computer programming and skills class with
SWICC during
the summer of 1997.

Proficient in Microsoft Office (Word, Excel, PowerPoint, Access), POS, Adobe
Reader, Internet Explorer, and WordPerfect. Completed a computer programming and
skills class with SWICC during the summer of 1997.
```

8. Test this version of your résumé by sending it to yourself and a friend. It is a good idea to use a few friends who have different operating systems or e-mail programs.

Attaching as .txt file:

1. Complete steps 1–4 from above.

2. Go to your e-mail program and attach the file you have just saved to an e-mail.

3. Your .txt résumé is now attached to the e-mail.

E-form: You may be asked to paste your résumé into an E-form.

1. Open the file you saved in the .txt format: *your_full_name_email_resume.txt*.

2. Click File and Page Setup and change left and right margins to 1.5 inch and the top and bottom to 1 inch. You are doing this so that no lines have more than 65 characters including spaces. This step ensures they fit nicely on most computer screens. You may need to clean up the document by taking care of any awkward spacing issues created after you change the margins.

3. Click File and Save As. Rename the file name to *your_full_name_uploadable_ resume.txt* and click OK.

A word of caution: When you post your résumé on a Web site, you should omit your references so that their names and contact information are not all over the Web.

■ RECOMMENDED FILE NAMES

For transforming your traditional résumé to an electronic version: *your_full_name_ electronicresume.doc*

For printing and sending to scan: *your_full_name_scannable_to_printresume.doc*

For e-mailing in the body of a message and as an attachment: *your_full_name_ email_resume.txt*

For E-forms: *your_full_name_uploadable_resume.txt*

Scannable version

Hailey N. Kenkel

2410 South Seminole Drive
Independence, MO 64057
(816) 210-6340
Haileykenkel@hotmail.com

OBJECTIVE

To obtain a challenging internship with The Kansas City Sports Commission in
Marketing or Event Coordination.

EDUCATION

Bachelor of Science, Double Major: Organizational Communication
May 2008
University of Missouri, Kansas City, Kansas City, Missouri

Classes to be completed by Spring 2005:
Promotion, Managerial Communication, Principles of Marketing, Sales and Sales
Management, Human Resource Management

Work 20–25 hours while attending school full-time
Computer Skills: Microsoft Word, Excel, Publisher, PowerPoint, Internet Explorer,
Access, Photoshop, Outlook, and Netscape Navigator

RELATED EXPERIENCE

Office Assistant
Health, Physical Education, Recreation, and Dance Department (HPERD)
University of Missouri, Kansas City, Kansas City, Missouri
August 2005 to Present
Answer phones and provide information or direct the caller to appropriate department.
Create flyers and posters informing students of University functions.
Create forms and programs for Professors in the Corporation Recreation Department.
Manage time and prioritize work to meet deadlines.
Communicate professionally with other campus departments through the phone, e-mails,
and letters.

Basketball Official
Missouri State High School Activities Association
Kansas City, Missouri
April 2005 to Present
Oversee play and sportsmanship of players, coaches, and fans at the High School level.
Consult with other officials, players, and coaches about regulations and review of rules.

Hailey N. Kenkel–page 2

Volunteer Assistant Basketball Coach
Youth Girls' Basketball Assistant Coach
Kansas City, Missouri
April 2005 to August 2005
Raised over $10,000 through presentations to companies, flyers, and benefits.
Coached 14 and under girls with ball handling, shooting skills; designed plays.
Participated in AAU (Amateur Athletic Union) Nationals in Orlando, Florida, placing thirteenth out of fifty teams.

ACTIVITIES/ORGANIZATIONS

American Marketing Association
Alpha Sigma Alpha Sorority
   Banner Co-Chair
   Social Committee
Student Senate
   Associate Member
UMKC Women's Basketball
Walk for Alzheimer's Volunteer
WIN for KC Event Volunteer
Kansas City Special Olympics
Campus Crusade
Team Leadership
Bristol Manner Volunteer
Adopt-A-Highway

62haileykenkel_email.resume

Hailey N. Kenkel

E-mailable version

2410 South Seminole Drive
Independence, MO. 64057
(816) 210-6340
Haileykenkel@hotmail.com

OBJECTIVE

To obtain a challenging internship with The Kansas City Sports Commission in
Marketing or Event Coordination.

EDUCATION

Bachelor of Science, Double Major: Organizational Communication

May 2008
University of Missouri - Kansas City, Kansas City, Missouri

Classes to be completed by Spring 2005:
Promotion, Managerial Communication, Principles of Marketing, Sales and Sales
Management, Human Resource Management

Work 20-25 hours while attending school full-time
Computer Skills: Microsoft Word, Excel, Publisher, PowerPoint, Internet Explorer,
Access, Photoshop, Outlook, and Netscape Navigator

RELATED EXPERIENCE

Office Assistant
Health, Physical Education, Recreation, and Dance Department (HPERD)
University of Missouri - Kansas City, Kansas City, Missouri

August 2005 to Present
Answer phones and provide information or direct the caller to appropriate
department.
Create flyers and posters informing students of University functions.
Create forms and programs for Professors in the Corporation Recreation Department.
Manage time and prioritize work to meet deadlines.
Communicate professionally with other campus departments through the phone,
e-mails, and letters.

Basketball Official
Missouri State High School Activities Association
Kansas City, Missouri

April 2005 to Present
Oversee play and sportsmanship of players, coaches, and fans at the High School
level.
Consult with other officials, players, and coaches about regulations and review of
rules.

Volunteer Assistant Basketball Coach
Youth Girls' Basketball Assistant Coach
Kansas City, Missouri

April 2005 to August 2005
Raised over $10,000 through presentations to companies, flyers, and benefits.
Coached 14 and under girls with ball handling, shooting skills, and designed plays.
Participated in AAU (Amateur Athletic Union) Nationals in Orlando, Florida, placing
13th.

62haileykenkel_email.resume.txt

ACTIVITIES/ORGANIZATIONS

American Marketing Association
Alpha Sigma Alpha Sorority
      Banner Co-Chair
      Social Committee
Student Senate
      Associate Member
UMKC Women's Basketball
Walk for Alzheimer's Volunteer
WIN For KC Event Volunteer
Kansas City Special Olympics
Campus Crusade
Team Leadership
Bristol Manner Volunteer
Adopt-A-Highway

PART TWO

2

Cover Letters

Your Cover Letter—
A Résumé's Introducer

Even the most professional résumé needs an introduction. We call it the cover (or application) letter. Targeting the employer's unique needs in this document is critical. Your first step is to find out what an employer deems crucial to the organization or position. Luckily, many employers have Web sites that clearly outline their preferred criteria. If a Web site is not readily available, you will use your well-developed phone skills to call and inquire about a position. In general, you need answers to the following questions:

- What are the title and department of the position you are filling (now or in the near future)?

- What are the name (with correct spelling) and title of the direct supervisor of the position?

- What are the major duties of the position, or what criteria are especially important for the position?

- Get the name and spelling of the person who supplies this information, because you may need it for your attention-getter. Graciously thank him or her for helping you.

Even if an employer has the information readily available online, an assertive applicant will call the employer to establish the initial contact.

Do I always need a cover letter?
Unless you are handing your résumé to an employer in person, such as at a job fair, you should have a cover letter. It introduces your résumé, which is as important as introducing yourself to someone you have never met. This document allows you to showcase your personality and own unique style.

Where do I start?
Most people prepare their résumé prior to their cover letter; if you have not done so, develop your résumé first. Before you prepare your first cover letter, complete the worksheet following this section. Having a worksheet containing concrete examples of material appropriate for your cover letter will streamline the process. You can also use this worksheet to prepare for an interview.

What format will I use?
The book provides examples of the cover letter and résumé as a pair so that you can visualize the two as a couple. Professionalism is critical to both documents. Notice that the headings or contact information on both documents complement each other when laid out side by side.

A new format referred to as the "T" or "two-column" letter provides one of the best formats for your letter. This format is easier to write and easier for the employer to read than traditional formats. One obstacle a writer has to overcome in the traditional format is reducing the use of "I" throughout the letter; this is easily accomplished in a "T" or "two-column" letter.

A brief reminder to analyze your audience when composing any business document is warranted at this point. Your employment documents (cover letter, résumé, and reference page) will usually be reviewed by both a screener (human resource professional or scanning program) and the individual who will be making the final hiring decision. The screener reviews hundreds of documents, so he or she is primarily interested in ensuring that applicants meet the basic requirements of the position; the person ultimately making the hiring decision will be digging deeper into your background and attributes. Your letter needs to meet the needs of both of these audiences by using a format that quickly identifies you as a candidate who possesses *all* of the minimum requirements, while also providing detail that clearly highlights your unique qualifications for the position.

While this format is relatively new, feedback from employers reviewing this format has been overwhelmingly positive. This format is featured on many of the top career advice Internet sites (MSN, Monster, Quintessential) but has not made its way into traditional texts yet. A few examples comparing traditional letters to the "T" format are also included for those of you not comfortable with the "T" format.

To whom should I address the letter?

Always find a contact name for your cover letter address. Ideally, this is the person who ultimately will be hiring for the position. Your second option is to send it to the human resource or personnel department. Either way, you will need to get the correct spelling of the individual and his or her exact title. The only exception to not using a personalized greeting is if the position is targeted to a blind post office box in which the employer is not identified.

Directly across from the proper person, you should identify the job you are targeting and where you found out about the position. Why? This clearly identifies the pile your letter will be placed in and replaces the bland opening many cover letters use to start their document. "Please consider this letter as my formal application for employment within your organization" really doesn't catch a reader's attention.

Since a cover letter is a persuasive document, you will follow the basic format of all persuasive communication. This includes an attention-getter, interest, desire or true conviction, and an action close.

Attention-getter

Your first obstacle is to get someone to read your letter rather than throw it away. As mentioned earlier, simply saying you are applying for a position is rather boring and will sound virtually identical to most other letters an employer will review. Instead, you should drop a name, show you have thoroughly researched an organization, indicate a strong interest in the product or service, or use a thought-provoking question or quote or creative clip art.

Since a picture is worth a thousand words, I have included samples of letters that demonstrate all four options.

- Drop a name—Meagan Platt.
- Show you have thoroughly researched an organization—Zach Peterman, Meagan Platt.
- Indicate a strong interest in the product or service—Leah Bostwick.
- Use a thought-provoking question or quote—Molly Stiens, Erica Espey, Mary K. Baumli.
- Use creative bullets—Molly Stiens, Hailey Kenkel, Zach Peterman.

Interest

Once you have caught the reader's attention, you will need a brief statement tying your attention-getter to your major attributes. Very often, this statement involves a reference to your résumé and a statement that you have outlined or highlighted how your skills meet the employer's needs. It is best to indirectly refer to your résumé. Rather than directly saying "I've enclosed my résumé for your review," you should say "My leadership skills as president of my fraternity are outlined in the enclosed résumé."

Desire (Conviction)

Now the work you spent (or will spend) preparing your worksheet will really pay off. Simply pick four to six items that you deem most critical to the position (based on your research), and describe concretely how you have demonstrated this skill. Start by labeling the two columns so that the reader can easily pick out what skills you are highlighting. The column on the left usually identifies the needs you are addressing, and the column on the right identifies your unique demonstration of this skill. Notice the specific examples used in the following samples. If an employer asks for oral communication skills, it is not enough to indicate you have passed a speech class. All college students can say this, so instead pinpoint a unique method of demonstrating your skills. For instance, "Excelled at facilitating team project meetings for 6–8 participants during my internship."

You have to *convince* the employer that they need to interview you for the position. Use the cover letter to highlight the accomplishments and transferable skills you included in your résumé. Ideally, the reader will be drawn to elements in your résumé while reading your cover letter.

Action Close

You will need to indicate that you are going to contact the reader either to set up an interview, check on the status of the position, or to discuss the position in more detail. Leaving the ball in the employer's court is *not* a good idea. Indicating you will be calling also makes it easier to get past a secretary. To say "Mr. Jones is expecting my call" is not a bluff but a valid statement, since you mentioned it in your cover letter. Indicate a general date, usually one to two weeks after having sent the letter. Close with a brief note of appreciation for taking the time to read your information.

After you have signed your name, you will also need to indicate that you have included a résumé after you type *Enclosure*.

How do I type the word "résumé" instead of "resume"?

You usually only have the word "résumé" once or twice in your cover letter. The easiest way to type the word "résumé" (with the accent marks) is to first type it wrong ("resum") so that the spelling function automatically will flag it as a misspelling by placing a red underline beneath the word. Right-click on the word and the list of words with accents will show up.

How do you get the fancy bullets used in several of the examples?

1. Go to Format and select Bullets and Numbering.
2. Click on type of bullet and select Customize and then Character or Picture.

If you've used Character, a Symbol box will open; select either Webdings or Wingdings as the font selection. It has some great options for bullets (i.e., ▥ ✝ ☎ ✆ ⊠ ➡ ⊕ ▮ ⚒ ☏ ⌂). Experiment with the font size of your characters after you have them all in place. You will generally have to increase their font size so that they are easy to interpret.

If you've used Picture, you'll next type the text of the type of picture you want into the search function (i.e., apple, basketball, Bible, computer, golf ball). Caution: You'll need to use a high-quality inkjet or laser printer to ensure that the crisp look of your graphic is professional.

3. After you have found an appropriate Character or Picture, select it by left-clicking on it and then selecting OK.
4. You may need to set the bullet positions. It works well to set the Bullet Indent to 0 and the Text position Tab space after and Indent both to 0.2"; now select OK.

Make sure your bullet looks ultraprofessional; a pinch of color or a unique design element often really enhances the visual effect of your letter.

P.S.

A sales technique frequently used in persuasive documents is a postscript. You may want to include this if you are seeking a position in a creative field or if it fits an organization that you are targeting.

■ COVER LETTER WORKSHEET

List several examples of how you have demonstrated as many of the skills as you can think of. Just a keyword or two is necessary. A few examples are given to get you started. Circle the skill or attribute your ad specifically requests because they are critical to include in your letter.

Attribute or Skill	Example 1	Example 2	Example 3
Written Communication	*Prepared exceptional business letters and reports in Business Communications course*		
Oral Communication	*Became comfortable presenting to small and large groups as campus recruiter*		
Teamwork (works well with others)	*Known as employee willing to pull my weight and always eager to help others*		
Problem Solver	*Identified problems while they still were small at McDonald's (tray placement)*		
Leadership	*Inspired the confidence of my faculty advisor as honor society president*		
Creativity	*Created theme "No Business like Mo Business" used at business fair*		
Strong Work Ethic	*Work 30 hours per week while going to school full-time*		
Education	*Completed 80 hours towards a degree in business including four accounting courses*		
Work Experience	*Two years of administrative support in a busy Human Resource office*		
Internship	*Completed Target's first class merchandising internship*		
Interpersonal Skills (relates well to others)	*Displays self-confidence and authority as Peer Advisor for 20 college freshmen*		
Honesty/Integrity	*Trusted to deposit cash at end of shift (up to $3,000)*		

Molly Stiens

Permanent Address:
123 South 10th Street
Fort Calhoun, NE 68023
(402) 468-5858

E-mail:
MStiens@hotmail.com
Mobile: (402) 650-8974

Local Address:
380 South Complex
Fremont, NE 68025
(402) 464-6106

November 18, 2005

Mr. Jerry Beach
Superintendent
Fort Calhoun Jr./Sr. High School
1506 Lincoln St.
Fort Calhoun, NE 68023

RE: Business Education teaching position

Dear Mr. Beach:

I was excited to hear from Patty Apple, your secretary, that there was an opportunity to be a teacher in the business education department. Developing skills in business and computers has been my forte. After looking at my résumé you will see that I meet the qualifications you are looking for.

You want someone:	I have:
Majoring in Business Education	Completed 131 hours toward my degree, including 13 business courses.
With computer skills	Successfully completed six computer courses working with Microsoft Office, Adobe Acrobat, and Dragon Naturally Speaking.
With oral communication skills	Comfortably presented to small and large groups in several of my classes and as a camp counselor. Fellow class members have commented on my professional speaking ability and sincere style.
Who possesses a strong work ethic	Worked 20 hours a week while attending school full-time and maintaining a 3.4 GPA.
With work experience	Experience in guest services working in a hotel for over one year. I worked with a hotel management computer program to make reservations and answer a 4-line phone system, in addition to resolving guest problems and complaints.

Mr. Beach, I am eager to discuss becoming a part of your distinguished school district. I will call next week to set up a time to meet with you at your convenience. Thank you for taking the time to review my qualifications.

I look forward to meeting with you,

Molly Stiens
Enclosure: Résumé

Molly Stiens

Permanent Address:		Local Address:
123 South 10th Street	E-mail:	380 South Complex
Fort Calhoun, NE 68023	Mstiens@hotmail.com	Fremont, NE 68025
(402) 468-5858	Mobile: (402) 650-8974	(402) 464-6106

Profile:

- Hardworking individual with a fun and enthusiastic attitude.
- Great leadership skills that are used to take initiative.
- Good use of time management skills used to set priorities.

- Full of fresh and inventive ideas.
- Excellent interpersonal and communication skills.
- Dedicated to helping others.
- Outstanding multitasking ability.

Education:

Bachelor of Science Degree with a major in Business Education   May 2006
University of Nebraska at Omaha   3.4/4.0 GPA
- Related business courses: Accounting I & II, Managerial Communications, Economics I & II, Digitools, Business Law, Principles of Marketing.
- Work 20 hours per week while registered full-time.
- Received six academic scholarships over the course of four years.

Computer Skills
- Microsoft Office: Excel, PowerPoint and Word, Internet Explorer, Hotel Management system

Work Experience:

Best Inn & Suites   Omaha, Nebraska   September 2004 – Present
  Guest Representative
- Ensure guest satisfaction with quick and easy check-in process for 25 – 60 guests per shift.
- Provide guests an after-check-in courtesy call to make sure they are comfortable.
- Work with a hotel management computer program to make reservations and answer a 4-line phone system.
- Close and balance cash drawer of $600.
- Resolve guest problems and complaints.

Blair Family YMCA   Blair, Nebraska   Summer 2005
  Camp Counselor
- Supervised and assisted in a variety of games and activities for 15 children, kindergarten through sixth grade.
- Chaperoned 10 field trips throughout the summer.
- Carried out a structured discipline procedure.
- Gained experience in planning and preparing impromptu activities.

Honors and Activities:

- Phi Eta Sigma National Honor Society Inducted April 2005
- National Society of Collegiate Scholars Inducted September 2005

- Accounting Society – 2004
- K.I.D.S. (Kind Individuals Dedicated to Students) – 2005

Hailey N. Kenkel

2410 South Seminole Drive
Independence, MO. 64057
(816) 210-6340
Hkenkel@hotmail.com

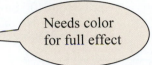

Needs color
for full effect

November 9, 2007

Ms. Tracie Dittimore   Re: Summer Internship
Administration
Kansas City Sports Commission and Foundation
1308 Pennsylvania
Kansas City, MO 64105

Dear Ms. Dittimore:

I was excited to hear about the opportunity for an internship at The Kansas City Sports Commission from one of your last summer interns, Molli Shelbi, and am very eager to discuss contributing to such an exceptional organization. After reviewing my résumé, I think you will find that my qualifications are what you are looking for.

You Want Someone With	**I . . .**
The talent to develop ideas	Designed a book cover for the Corporate Recreation Department at UMKC, which is used as a part of an everyday curriculum for 200 students each semester.
Thorough knowledge of sports	Played basketball at UMKC and coached a fourth- and fifth-grade girls' basketball team. Been a basketball official for five years and a Missouri Certified Official for two years.
The ability to deal effectively with the public	Deal with 25 faculty and students on an everyday basis in a professional setting. As a basketball official, conversed with players, coaches, and parents in difficult situations.
The capability to develop flyers, press releases, and correspondences	Excel at designing letters and flyers using Microsoft Publisher; raised over $10,000 for youth basketball team. Frequently selected by faculty to create posters and bulletin boards informing students of UMKC functions and events.

Ms. Dittimore, I am very excited about the opportunity to work for The Kansas City Sports Commission as an intern. My experience, educational background, and love of all sports will make me a perfect fit for this internship. I will call you on November 29 to check on the status of your selection process. Thank you for your time and consideration.

Sincerely,

Hailey N. Kenkel
Enclosure: Résumé

Hailey N. Kenkel

2410 South Seminole Drive
Independence, MO 64057
(816) 210-6340
Hkenkel@hotmail.com

OBJECTIVE

To obtain a challenging internship with The Kansas City Sports Commission in Marketing or Event Coordination.

EDUCATION

Bachelor of Science Degree, Double Major: Organizational Communication   **May 2008**
University of Missouri - Kansas City

- **Classes to be completed by Spring 2005:**
  - ▶ Promotion
  - ▶ Principles of Marketing
  - ▶ Human Resource Management
  - ▶ Managerial Communication
  - ▶ Sales and Sales Management

- Work 20–25 hours while attending school full-time
- **Computer Skills:** Microsoft Word, Excel, Publisher, PowerPoint, Internet Explorer, Access, Photoshop, Outlook, and Netscape Navigator

RELATED EXPERIENCE

Health, Physical Education, Recreation, and Dance Department (HPERD)
UMKC - Kansas City, Missouri   **August 2005 to Present**
Office Assistant
- Answer phones and provide information or direct the caller to appropriate department
- Create flyers and posters informing students of University functions
- Create forms and programs for Professors in the Corporation Recreation Department
- Manage time and prioritize work to meet deadlines
- Communicate professionally with other campus departments through the phone, e-mails, and letters

Missouri State High School Activities Association
Kansas City, Missouri   **April 2005 to Present**
Basketball Official
- Oversee play and sportsmanship of players, coaches, and fans at the High School level
- Consult with other officials, players, and coaches about regulations and review of rules

Youth Girls' Basketball Assistant Coach
Kansas City, Missouri   **April 2005 to August 2005**
Volunteer Assistant Basketball Coach
- Raised over $10,000 through presentations to companies, flyers, and benefits
- Coached 14 and under girls with ball handling and shooting skills, and designed plays
- Participated in AAU (Amateur Athletic Union) Nationals in Orlando, Florida, placing 13th

ACTIVITIES/ORGANIZATIONS

- American Marketing Association
- Alpha Sigma Alpha Sorority
  - Banner Co-Chair
  - Social Committee
- Student Senate
  - Associate Member
- UMKC Women's Basketball

- Walk for Alzheimers Volunteer
- WIN For KC Event Volunteer
- Kansas City Special Olympics
- Campus Crusade
- Team Leadership
- Bristol Manner Volunteer
- Adopt-A-Highway

When cover letters are e-mailed they should be very concise. The title of the position *and* your name should be included in the subject line. Even though the letter is short, it should include an attention-getter and action closing.

To: Aredden@gentledental.com

From: Emily Kisker

Subject: Dental Hygienist Position (#8484) Résumé from Emily Kisker

Dear Dr. Redden:

Chloe recommended I forward my résumé to your office immediately for consideration for your dental hygienist position.

After reviewing your practice's Web site and talking to your office manager over the phone, I find my skills fit well with your need for another dental hygienist in your growing operation. My AS degree in Dental Hygiene will be completed December of this year, and I look forward to putting my well-honed skills to work.

My résumé is attached to this message per the instructions on your Web site. I welcome the opportunity to talk to you about joining your team to help provide gentle dental care to your clients. I'll check on the status of your opening early next week.

Sincerely,

Emily Kisker
xxx-xxx-xxxx
Ekisker@hotmail.com

Résumé attached

Include your contact Information after your name since this format doesn't include your personal letterhead. Your e-mail address doesn't have to be unlinked.

Emily Kisker

711 Torrance Circle ▪ Boise, ID zipcode ▪ (xxx) xxx-xxxx ▪ Ekisker@hotmail.com

PROFILE

Dental Hygienist with a friendly chair-side manner. Excel at providing gentle yet thorough cleanings. Skilled at persuading clients to take better care of their teeth and gums. Frequently requested by patients.

EDUCATION

Associate of Science Degree: Dental Hygienist   December 2006
Apollo College, Boise, Idaho   Overall GPA: 3.6/4.0
- 100% of educational expenses self-funded through scholarships and working 15 hours per week
- Coursework provided exceptional training in clinical and diagnostic testing, peridontology, dental materials, and clinical dental hygiene.
- Licensed in the state of Idaho.

RELATED WORK EXPERIENCE

Gentle Dental Care ~ Boise, Idaho   June 1999 – Present
Dental Assistant   (November 2000 – Present)
- Responsible for chair-side assisting with patients ranging in age from 2 – 90.
- Clean up assistant/hygienist rooms after each procedure.
- Sterilize instruments and develop X-rays for 4 rooms.
- Work in lab on impressions and models of teeth.

Secretarial Assistant   (June 1999 – Present)
- Prepare patient charts.
- Confirm appointments every day for approximately 40 patients.
- Manage computer records and file charts and insurance claims.
- Correspondence representative for office when calling outside contacts.
- Perform receptionist duties and other office tasks.

Apollo College ~ Boise, Idaho   Fall 2004
Peer Advisor for Freshman Seminar-Marketing/Management Department
- Selected by faculty to help 20 freshmen adjust to college through instruction and academic advisement.

COMPUTER SKILLS

Microsoft: (Word, PowerPoint, Access)   Excel - Microsoft Certified 2002
Dragon Speech Recognition, Internet Explorer

HONORS & ACTIVITIES

Campus Crusade for Christ
- Attended Summer Project in Myrtle Beach, SC ~ Chosen as Women's Time Leader for 50 females
- Selected twice to give motivational speech for 250 peers
- Skits/Ice Breakers Committee
- Mentor for a younger woman

Phi Eta Sigma (freshman) Honor Society

Dean's Honor Roll (all semesters)
CPR Certified by American Heart Association (August 2003)
Member of Wind Symphony-top honor band
Kappa Kappa Psi Honorary Music Fraternity
- Service Committee
- Academic Award (3.5 – 4.0 GPA)

Participated in Intramural Volleyball
Basic Knowledge of American Sign Language (ASL)

MEAGAN E. PLATT

Local: 30 West Dunn
Maytown, IA 03015
(933) 496-0001

plattm456@none.net

Permanent: 933 Sanford St.
Fredrick, IA 03116
(933) 937-1298

November 5, 2005

Mr. Rick Hansen   Re: Summer 2006 Internship
Supervisor
Federal Reserve Bank
925 Grand Boulevard
Kansas City, MO 64198

Dear Mr. Hansen:

Your Kirkwood Community College career fair representative, Jeff Owen, spoke to me about the Management Career Track Internship opportunity at the Federal Reserve Bank. A friend of mine, Jamie Knierim, also talked very highly of her summer 2005 internship with the Fed and encouraged me to apply. It is my understanding that this internship will challenge students through diverse projects and "hands-on" experience. In reviewing my résumé, you will find that I possess all the needed skills to be a successful intern and an asset to your business.

You Need Someone With:	**I Have:**
◆ Analytical ability	◆ Used technical analysis to evaluate stocks and calculated company budgets in courses taken at Kirkwood Community College
◆ Communication skills	◆ Gained valuable writing skills in Honors Composition and have given many effective oral presentations individually and with groups; poised presentation style
◆ Initiative	◆ Been driven to become successful in my career area by achieving a 4.0 GPA and being inducted into four honor societies on campus; step forward to help a group meet a goal when the opportunity arises
◆ Leadership	◆ Exercised leadership as Treasurer of Alpha Sigma Alpha Sorority and Vice President of Pre-Law Society; known as a leader who projects self-confidence, authority, and enthusiasm
◆ Creativity	◆ Devised attractive advertisements for the local newspaper and seasonal window displays as an employee of Bedford Building Supply

Mr. Hansen, my experience and educational background would make me a perfect fit for this internship. I will call you on November 15 to arrange an interview at your convenience to discuss my skills and qualifications for the Management Career Track Internship. My Thanksgiving break from school, November 22–26, would be an ideal time for me to visit your prestigious organization.

Sincerely,

Meagan E. Platt
Enclosure: Résumé

MEAGAN E. PLATT

Local: 30 West Dunn
Maytown, IA 03015
(933) 496-0001

plattm456@none.net

Permanent: 933 Sanford St.
Fredrick, IA 03116
(933) 937-1298

PROFILE

- ♦ Proficient in Microsoft Office (Word, Excel, PowerPoint, Publisher), QuickBooks Pro 2001, Adobe Reader 6.0
- ♦ Excellent leader willing to take initiative
- ♦ Dedicated student willing to go the extra mile to turn in excellent work
- ♦ Recipient of Presidential Scholarship, which is only given to 10 students out of 2,000 each year

EDUCATION

Bachelor of Science Degree with majors in Corporate Finance and Financial Services   Graduation: May 2007
- ♦ Kirkwood Community College, Cedar Rapids, Iowa   4.0/4.0 Cumulative GPA
- ♦ Education self-funded through scholarships, grants, and part-time employment

WORK EXPERIENCE

Judicial Liaison   Cedar Rapids, Iowa   August 2004 – Present
Kirkwood Community College Student Affairs Office
- ♦ Ensure understanding of the judicial process to students appearing before Student-Faculty Discipline Committee. Maintain a database of all case statistics and compile series of graphs over yearly trends. Trusted to uphold confidentiality between students and public.

Salesperson   Conrad, Iowa   May 2003 – Present
Bedford Building Supply
- ♦ Balance cash drawer and deposit cash in amounts averaging $3,000. Create window displays and prepare newspaper advertisements. Assist customers with complaints and look up information with QuickBooks Pro. Order and maintain hardware inventory averaging $35,000. Purchased new shelving and organized new floor plans to expand inventory. Demonstrated problem-solving skills. Installing merchandise scanner system and helping with changeover to new hardware supplier.

LEADERSHIP ACTIVITIES

- ♦ Alpha Sigma Alpha Sorority: Treasurer, 2005 ($18,000 budget) and Guard, 2004
- ♦ Pre-law Society: Vice President, 2004 and Secretary, 2003
- ♦ Association of Financial Professionals: Member Spring, 2005
- ♦ Student Senate: Lobbied in Des Moines, Iowa, for higher education, 2005

- ♦ Perrin Hall Council: President, 2004 and Treasurer, 2003
- ♦ Financial Management Association International: Honor Society Member, Recruitment and Social Chair, 2004, FMA Leaders' Conference - Chicago delegate, tutor finance students, and give investment presentation to freshmen groups

RECOGNITIONS AND HONORS

- ♦ Sigma Pi Sigma Presidential Scholar Full in-state tuition, room, and board
- ♦ Mortar Board: National Senior Honor Society, Fund-raising Chair, "Top 10 Sophomore Award"
- ♦ National Society of Collegiate Scholars: Academic Honor Society
- ♦ Cook/Imes Distinguished Scholarship

- ♦ Delta Mu Delta National Honor Society: Top 20% of business students
- ♦ Phi Eta Sigma National Freshmen Honor Society
- ♦ Cardinal Key National Honor Society
- ♦ Order of Omega: Greek Honor Society B.A.N.G. (Being a New Greek) group leader

Treyton Burch

Permanent Address
801 Cosby
Oklahoma City, OK 73102
405-992-4642

treytonburch14@hotmail.com

Local Address
219 West 2nd Street
Langston, OK 73050
405-466-7461

January 14, 2006

Dr. Sam Shamsi
Director, GIS & IT Division
ATS-Chester Engineers, Inc.
Airside Business Park
250 Airside Drive
Moon Township, PA 15108-3195

Re: GIS technical support internship as
advertised on GIS Job Clearinghouse

Dear Dr. Shamsi:

I was extremely excited to hear from Bob Black that ATS-Chester Engineers, Inc. has a GIS technical support internship opportunity available. After reviewing my résumé you will find that I would be a great asset to your company as an intern.

You require:

- Associates degree or two-year equivalent

- Strong working knowledge of ArcView or ArcGIS software and database software

- Experience with Windows 2000/XP, Microsoft Office, and spreadsheet software

- Digitizing experience

I:

- Will graduate from Langston University with a Bachelor of Science degree in Geography in April 2006

- Have Class experience which has provided me with a strong working knowledge of ArcView, ArcGIS, ArcCatalog, ArcToolbox, and spreadsheet software

- Frequently used Windows and Microsoft Office to create letters, budget spreadsheets, and newsletters as a Delta Chi Fraternity officer

- Used both on-screen digitizing and a digitizing tablet in my GIS courses

Mr. Shamsi, I will contact you toward the end of January to discuss a time that is convenient for you so that we may discuss what I can offer as an intern. Thank you for your time, and I look forward to talking with you.

Sincerely,

Treyton Burch

Enclosure: Résumé

Treyton Burch

Permanent Address	treytonburch14@hotmail.com	**Local Address**
801 Cosby		219 West 2nd Street
Oklahoma City, OK 73102		Langston, OK 73050
405-992-4642		405-466-7461

OBJECTIVE

A technical support internship for ATS-Chester Engineers, Inc.

EDUCATION

- Bachelor of Science Degree   April 2006
  Major: Geography   Minor: General Business
- Langston University, Langston, Oklahoma
- Computer Skills: Windows 2000/XP, Microsoft Office, ArcGIS, ArcView, ArcCatalog, ArcToolbox, Digitizing

RELATED EXPERIENCE

Delta Chi, International Social Fraternity   Langston, Oklahoma
    President   January 2003 – April 2004
Elected for two terms. Throughout span managed average chapter size of 60 men, $70,000 budget, organized effective and timely chapter meetings, and provided leadership retreats. Used delegation to assign tasks to executive members for weekly assignments where follow-up meetings were held to view completion status. Recruited an Alumni Board of Trustees with 8 officers, a 10-officer Housing Corporation, and Alumni Association with 3 officers to assist the chapter.

    Vice President   January 2002 – December 2002
Managed a committee system with 12 chairs. Held committee chair meetings where delegation was used to assign tasks. Directed two strategic planning retreats to establish goals and objectives for the chapter.

    Associate Member Counselor   May 2004 – December 2004
Developed associate members to become active members of the chapter. Held weekly meetings where workshops were presented to motivate and educate members on fraternity history, time-management, expectations, chapter operations, and other essentials important to prepare one for the business world.

Cascone's Italian Restaurant   Oklahoma City, Oklahoma   January 1998 – March 2003
    Busboy/Banquet Server/Host
Used creativity to set up banquet room for special events, assisted with customer needs, assigned duties to wait staff, trained new employees, managed sales, motivated employees, and handled customer service.

Mac's Soccer Shack   Oklahoma City, Oklahoma   October 1999 – August 2000
    Retail Assistant
Assisted with day-to-day operations to manage a soccer retail store. Managed cash register, prepared a bank deposit at closing, purchased orders from manufacturers, and monitored inventory. Used successful negotiating to close team sales with soccer clubs.

HONORS AND ACTIVITIES

Leadership Conferences
Delta Chi International Convention – 2004
NIC Alcohol Summit – 2003
Team Leadership Conference – 2003
Mid-America Greek Conference Association – 2003
Personal Leadership Retreat – 2003
Delta Chi Leadership Conference – 2002, 2004

Awards
Delta Chi Fraternity 2004 Best Active Member
Delta Chi Fraternity 2003 Best Active Member
Team Leadership 2003 Outstanding Leader
Team Leadership 2002 Emerging Leader
NIC Alcohol Summit Graduate – February 2003
Delta Chi Fraternity Brotherhood Award – 2002 – 2004

Word Count: 387

LEAH BOSTWICK

3033 State Street
Sandusky, OH 69987
Phone (991) 622-7944
leahb@ask.net

April 3, 2006

Mr. Pete Sully
Human Resources Manager
Pixar Animation Studios
1200 Park Avenue
Emeryville, CA 94608   Re: Animator for a feature film as shown on your Web site

Dear Mr. Sully:

After watching *Toy Story*, I could never look at my stuffed koala the same way again. Pixar's animated movies made me feel like *Alice in Wonderland*, eager to explore just how deep the rabbit hole goes. Ever since *Toy Story*, it has been a dream of mine to work at Pixar, creating stories that challenge imaginations and open up wondrous possibilities. I am eager to add my brand of creativity to the magic that is "Pixar."

You need someone	I have
◆ To create the motions, gestures, and expressions of three-dimensional computer graphics characters and objects	◆ Experience in Flash MX and Microsoft Paintbrush creating characters in short animated movies
◆ With an art background, who shows a thorough understanding of motion, weight, balance, texture, and form	◆ Completed 62 hours toward a degree in Interactive Digital Media (Visual Imaging) at University of Cincinatti, which includes drawing, painting, and imaging courses
◆ With proven storytelling skills and ability to use acting skills to bring characters to life as well as clearly communicate simple ideas with which an audience can empathize	◆ Actively participated in storytelling competitions since the age of nine and been involved in the performing arts since the age of five
◆ Ability to work collaboratively	◆ Worked successfully with debating team members to emerge as district champions

Mr. Sully, I am enthusiastic about the possibility of becoming a member of the Pixar team. I will contact you next week to arrange a meeting time that will be convenient for you so that we can discuss my qualifications and how I can help expand Pixar's horizons *"To Infinity and beyond."*

Sincerely,

Leah Bostwick
Enclosure: Résumé

LEAH BOSTWICK

3033 State Street, Sandusky, OH 69987
Phone (991) 622-7944 - leahb@ask.net

OBJECTIVE

To obtain the animator position at Pixar Animation Studios.

SUMMARY OF SKILLS

- **Communication skills (verbal and written)** – Prepared meeting minutes as secretary of Interact Club and presented ideas and reports to members.
- **Honesty/Integrity** – Trusted with the funds when elected as treasurer of two separate organizations (Leadership Society and Interact Club).
- **Teamwork skills** – Worked cooperatively with debate team members to win district-level tournament, and collaborated in making decisions as a board member of several organizations.
- **Strong work ethic** – Participated actively in projects organized by the Interact Club and demonstrated required dedication to attain position of Student Body Leader at high school.

EDUCATION

Bachelor of Science ~ University of Cincinnati, Cincinnati, Ohio   August 2006
Double Major: Interactive Digital Media (Computer Science and Visual Imaging Concentrations)   GPA ~ 3.42/4.0
Minor in General Business and Computer Science

COMPUTER SKILLS

Microsoft software: Word, Excel, Outlook, PowerPoint   Operating systems: Windows, Unix, Linux
Computer languages: Java and C   Other: Internet Explorer, Netscape, Flash MX,
                                                                      Dreamweaver

WORK EXPERIENCE

Kiwanis Society Social Worker   **Seremban, Negeri Sembilan, Malaysia**   **Nov. – Dec. 2003**
  Tutored 20 kids aged 3 – 6 with Down syndrome. Taught them basic skills such as reading, speaking, and identifying objects. Demonstrated creativity and patience while instructing.

Private Computer Tutor   **Seremban, Negeri Sembilan, Malaysia**   **June – Oct. 2003**
  Taught student basic computer skills such as computer software (Microsoft Word), e-mail, and Internet surfing.

Choral Speaking Assistant coach   **Ipoh, Perak, Malaysia**   **March – May 2003**
  Assisted choral speaking (poetry recitation) coach to train a group of 40 high school students in choral speaking skills. Prepared verses for the team and taught proper choral speaking mannerisms. Team placed 2nd in the Kinta II district.

HONORS AND ACTIVITIES

- Appointed Student Body Leader over 20 girls in high school
- Vice President of English Language Society
- Secretary/Treasurer of Interact Club in high school
- Best Speaker in Kinta II district debating tournament (Muhammad Wira Cup)

- Dean's list (3.5 – 4.0 GPA) at INTI College Malaysia
- Led Choral speaking team to 2nd placing in Kinta II district
- First speaker of the winning debating team (Jalil Cup)

Erica Espey

515 W. 11th St. Apt. 15
Enid, OK 73702
(502) 592-5758
eespey@osu.edu

April 4, 2005

Ms. Terri Cooper
Ladies Professional Golf Association
ATTN: Finance & Administration
100 International Golf Drive
Daytona Beach, FL 32124

Re: Business Tournament Affairs
Internship at www.lpga.com

Dear Ms. Cooper:

"I try to learn from everyone. I look at their strengths and ask myself, 'What can I do better?'"
These words by Annika Sorenstam, one of the LPGA's most renowned golfers, also ring true for
me. I am always looking for a challenge and am eager to improve myself. Working in the LPGA
will give me the opportunity to learn from the best in the business. After reviewing my résumé,
you will find it beneficial to have me as an intern.

You Want Someone Who	I Have
• Is enrolled in or has completed his or her junior year in an accredited college or university	• Completed my junior year at Oklahoma State University
• Has a cumulative GPA of 3.0 or better	• A cumulative GPA of 3.71 while majoring in business
• Works well in a team environment	• Been a part of the Oklahoma State Golf Team for two years; participated in intramural college teams as well as high school varsity basketball and golf teams
• Exhibits good communication skills	• Successfully completed Managerial Communications class, which focuses on business letters, résumés, and formal presentations
• Has solid leadership skills	• Facilitated team meetings and contacted coaches to coordinate tournaments for the Oklahoma State Golf Team

Ms. Cooper, I am excited to have the opportunity to discuss working for the LPGA and learn from
people that I have looked up to for years. I will be in touch with you on Thursday, April 15, to check on
the status of my application and answer any questions you may have.

Sincerely,

Erica Espey

Enclosure: Résumé

P.S.: My family will be visiting your area for a family reunion in May. Would this be a good time to
meet?

Erica Espey

515 W. 11th St. Apt. 15, Enid, OK 73702 (502) 592-5758
eespey@osu.edu

OBJECTIVE

To obtain a summer internship with the LPGA in Tournament Business Affairs.

EDUCATION

Bachelor of Science in Business Management   December 2006
Oklahoma State University, Stillwater, Oklahoma   GPA 3.71/4.0
- Business Courses to be complete by Summer 2005
  - Managerial Communications   - Accounting I & II
  - Management Process and Behavior   - Economics I & II
- 60% of education paid for with academic scholarships and working 20 hours per week

WORK EXPERIENCE

Oklahoma State High School Activities Association – Southern Oklahoma   November 2004 – Present
Basketball Official
- Supervise play and sportsmanship of players, coaches, and fans at middle school and high schools
- Enhancing ability to negotiate with other officials, teams, and coaches
- Completed two certification exams, earned high marks on evaluations

Kawasaki Motors Manufacturing Corp. USA – Oklahoma City, Oklahoma   Summer 2004
Factory Laborer
- Collaborated with a team of four to file and prepare engine parts for assembly
- Documented and provided hourly and daily quality and quantity data to supervisor
- Selected by supervisor to inspect quality of work for peer team members

Hy-Vee, Inc. – Tulsa, Oklahoma   August 1999 – August 2003
Checker/Stocker
- Assisted customers with needs such as finding items, prices, and checking out
- Inventoried products quarterly
- Handled $1,000+ cash daily and helped audit cash registers and safe
- Improved customer service skills

HONORS & ACTIVITIES

- Oklahoma State Women's Golf Club-Captain
- Oklahoma Women's Golf Association Scholarship
- KMA/KKBZ Sportscasters Club Scholarship
- National Society for Collegiate Scholars
- Community Betterment Youth Leader
- Nominated for United States Achievement Academy

- Duke Nuckolls Memorial Scholarship
- Van McNeil Memorial Scholarship
- Lydia L. Stickerod Scholarship
- OSU Honor's Scholarship
- HPERD Scholarship
- President's and Dean's Honor Roll (all semesters)
- Oklahoma State Intramurals

COMPUTER SKILLS

- Microsoft Software: Word, Excel, PowerPoint, Outlook, FrontPage
- Other Software: Windows, Quicken Deluxe, Internet Explorer

"All the so-called 'secrets of success' will not work unless you do." – Author Unknown

Zach Peterman

331 North B Avenue
Boulder, CO 80306
(303) 441-8484
zlpete@mschi.net

April 4, 2006

Mr. Russel Martin   Re: Campus Crusade for Christ Internship
Payroll Services
Campus Crusade for Christ
Lake Hart Drive
Orlando, FL 63212

Dear Mr. Martin:

I am excited to learn about an internship with Campus Crusade for Christ. I agree with Crusade's slogan of "turning lost students into Christ-centered laborers." This objective makes me eager to begin working in an atmosphere that has such a great goal and mission. After a review of my résumé, I think you will find me to be a worthy candidate for this internship.

You Need Someone With	I Have
✠ A belief in the mission of campus crusade	Spent many hours working with and for Campus Crusade in Boulder, Colorado; possess a strong belief in the values and mission of this important organization
✠ A strong work ethic	Helped on the farm since an early age, learning the value of "doing a job right"
✠ Excellent communication skills	Worked as a technology assistant where I developed and demonstrated skills needed to troubleshoot problems in a patient, professional manner
✠ Strong business knowledge	Applied theories from marketing and management courses working as a persuasive sales representative at Watson Fireworks; able to be assertive without being overly aggressive

Mr. Martin, I am excited about this opportunity to work for Campus Crusade for Christ as an intern. I will contact you on April 10 to discuss more thoroughly this opportunity for an internship and my qualifications for it. Thank you for taking the time to look at my résumé.

Sincerely,

Zach Peterman
Enclosure: Résumé

Zach Peterman

331 North B Avenue – Boulder, Colorado 80306
(303) 441-8484 – zlpete@mschi.net

OBJECTIVE

To obtain a summer internship with Campus Crusade for Christ.

EDUCATION

Bachelor of Science Degree   December 2006
Double Major in Business and Marketing Management; Minor in Coaching   GPA 3.88/4.0
University of Colorado, Boulder, Colorado
- 100% of education funded through academic scholarships and 10-hour-a-week work component.
- Computer Skills: Microsoft Office (Word, Excel, Access), Dreamweaver, Internet

RELATED EXPERIENCE

Campus Crusade for Christ Leadership   Boulder, Colorado   **2004 – 2005**
- o Outreach Team - Evangelism of 4 Spiritual Laws and conducted spiritual surveys.
- o Prayer Team - Meet weekly for prayer.
- o Setup Team - Set up music equipment and chairs for weekly meeting.

WORK EXPERIENCE

Watson Fireworks   Denver, Colorado   **Summer 2004 & 2005**
- Sold $3,500 worth of fireworks during a three-week period.
- Assisted in minimizing shoplifting by conducting surveillance during store hours.
- Coordinated and arranged shelf displays of fireworks.
- Managed two other employees by supervising and instructing them in the proper manner of selling fireworks.

Colorado Springs High School   Colorado Springs, Colorado   **Summer 2003**
- Assembled desktop computers from scratch.
- Installed and utilized Microsoft Office and antivirus software.
- Encountered and solved miscellaneous software and technical problems.

Rolf Farms   Colorado Springs, Colorado   **May 2000 – Aug. 2004**
- Managed production and marketing of swine, sweet corn, and grain.
- Expanded production in all three areas to increase efficiency and overall profits.
- Administered financial records and performed labor – walking beans and planting crops.

HONORS & ACTIVITIES

- Webmaster for 2003 Absolutely No Frills Conference
- Member of American Marketing Association (AMA)
- Delta Mu Delta (business honor society)

- Presidential Scholarship Winner
- Sigma Pi Sigma (Presidential Scholar Society)
- Humane Society Volunteer

Serena Troshynski

Local Address:
1210 Fox Rd. Apt. 4
Louiseville, KY 40292
(502) 852-0629   STro@hotmail.com

Permanent Address:
1311 North Dewey
Boston, MA 02115
(617) 497-2214

November 16, 2006

Mr. Joseph Ross   Re: Paralegal Opening
Attorney
Ross, Tobin & Adkins
925 Grand Boulevard
Boston, MA 02115

Dear Mr. Ross:

After completing an AA degree in paralegal studies at the University of Louisville, I'm ready to move back to my hometown to start my career. After thoroughly researching firms in the Boston area, I am convinced your establishment is truly one of the best. In reviewing my résumé, you will find that I am a hard worker and fast learner and possess all the skills you want in a paralegal.

You Need Someone With:	I Have:
• Proven leadership ability	• Exercised leadership as manager of a community swimming center and as a player on the University of Louisville's women's basketball team; known as a person of high integrity.
• Creativity	• Used a variety of methods needed to find an answer to any issue; willing to think outside the box when researching applicable case law.
• Initiative and proven expertise in the paralegal field	• Maintained a 4.0 GPA while practicing 20+ hours in a collegiate sport and have been selected to a number of honor societies.
• Well-developed communication skills	• Used an array of communication skills needed to conduct business in a fast-paced insurance agency, and developed additional skills through class projects and presentations.
• Exceptional analytical ability	• Applied problem-solving skills daily by evaluating a case from all angles to devise a variety of approaches needed to arrive at the optimal solution.

Mr. Ross, I am excited about the career possibilities available at Ross, Tobin & Adkins. I will contact you on November 29 to discuss the details of the internship and answer any questions about my qualifications. Thank you for taking the time to review my résumé.

Sincerely,

Serena Troshynski
Enclosure: Résumé

Serena Troshynski

Local Address:
1210 Fox Rd. Apt. 4
Louisville, KY 40292
(502) 852-0629

STro@hotmail.com

Permanent Address:
1311 North Dewey
Boston, MA 02115
(617) 497-2214

PROFILE

- Earned highest GPA in cohort enrolled in Paralegal Studies program.
- Possess excellent ability to research and prepare written memos, briefs, and reports that are accurate, concise, and thorough.
- Known as "Computer Guru"; enjoy searching for information; comfortable with Microsoft (Word, PowerPoint, Excel, Access) and many Internet search engines.
- Able to both pay attention to detail and see the "big picture."

EDUCATION

Associate of Arts in Paralegal Studies from University of Louisville   May 2008
Earned 4.0 GPA while playing on women's basketball team and taking 15 – 17 credit hours.

Highlight of courses most applicable to your law office:

- Legal Research & Writing (9 hours)
- Litigation (6 hours)
- Business Law
- Real Estate Law
- Contracts and Torts (6 hours)
- Wills, Estates, and Trusts
- Family Law
- Professional Ethics

WORK EXPERIENCE

Hughes Insurance Agency   Boston, Massachusetts   Summer 2006
Insurance Office Assistant

> Processed quotes for new customers by request over the phone or in person. Amended auto and home quotes as needed. Documented payments, requotes, claims, adjustments, and cancellations. Performed clerical work by answering the phone, sending faxes, filing, responding to e-mails, and answering questions of the clients. Developed the ability to multitask in a fast-paced environment.

YMCA Swimming Pool   Boston, Massachusetts   Summers 2003 – 2006
Manager (Summer 2002)

> Supervised seven employees and three substitute guards. Tracked and deposited daily monetary transactions. Organized Red Cross swimming lessons for 40+ children. Developed good interpersonal skills as a result of many interactions with children and parents. Designated cleaning duties and evaluated employee work. Instructor for private lessons.

Lifeguard (Summers 2001 – 2004)

> Monitored swimming areas to maintain safety of clientele. Rescued swimmers in danger of drowning and regularly administered first aid. Inspected facilities for unsafe conditions. Resolved public relations and pool issues. Responsible for all patrons whether in the water or on deck.

Miller Brother's Ranch Inc.   Boston, Massachusetts   Since age 12
Farm Hand

> Operate different types of machinery based on the task. Maintain facilities by building or repairing. Use physical labor while working livestock and repairing machinery or fences. Exercise problem-solving skills daily.

HONORS / ACTIVITIES

- National Federation of Paralegal Associations
- National Society of Collegiate Scholars
- Wendy's High School Heisman National Finalist
  - 6 women finalists/13,000 nominations nationwide
  - Excellence in academics, athletics, and community service
- Presidential Honor Roll
- Campus Crusade for Christ
- Phi Eta Sigma Honor Society

Emily Walker

303 Barnard Street
Warrensburg, MO 64461

emilyw@mail.nwmissouri.edu

1211 N. Prettyman St.
Harrisonville, MO 64701

March 27, 2005

Mr. Mike Murff
Human Resources Generalist
Hy-Vee Pharmacy
2000 East 95th St.
Kansas City, MO 64141

RE: Pharmacy Technician

Dear Mr. Murff:

"The most important single ingredient in the formula of success is knowing how to get along with people." When it comes to the importance of communication in the workforce, I think former president Theodore Roosevelt said it best. Communication is a very important aspect of this position, and the experience I have makes us a perfect match. In reviewing my résumé, you will find that I have the attributes that would make me an asset to your department.

Your Position Requirements	**My Qualifications**
• Good working knowledge of MS Project, Word, Excel	• Successfully completed detailed tasks and layouts using Microsoft Project, Word, and Excel
• Excellent communication, organizational, administrative, and interpersonal skills	• Four years' experience in organizing workload, performing different tasks with no margin for error, and learning to communicate effectively both verbally and in writing
• Commitment to outstanding customer service	• Five years' experience in customer service has provided me with the ability to work well with customers of all ages and dispositions
• Time-management skills and the ability to handle multiple tasks in a busy pharmacy	• Participate in three on-campus organizations while maintaining a 3.7/4.0 GPA

Mr. Murff, I am enthusiastic about discussing becoming one of the many employees who bring their knowledge and expertise to Hy-Vee's Pharmacy every day. I will contact you by April 4 to arrange a meeting at your convenience to discuss my qualifications for the position of Pharmacy Technician.

Sincerely,

Emily Walker

Enclosure: Résumé

Emily Walker

303 Barnard Street Warrensburg, MO 64461	emilyw@mail.nwmissouri.edu	1211 N. Prettyman St. Harrisonville, MO 64701

Key Strengths

OBJECTIVE

Pharmacy Technician

EDUCATION

Associate of Arts in General Studies   December 2006
Central Missouri State University, Warrensburg, Missouri   GPA 3.7/4.00
- Financed 100% of education through scholarships and summer employment
- Certified Pharmacy Technician (CPhT) until December 2008
- Courses related to internship to be completed by Summer 2005

Business Communications	Medical Terminology
Applied Psychology	Accounting I & II
Using Computers	Mgt. Processes & Behavior

Goal oriented

PROFESSIONAL EXPERIENCE

Gillen Pharmacy   **Harrisonville, Missouri**   **June 2000 – Present**

<u>Pharmacy Aide</u>
- Assist Pharmacist in a retail pharmacy. Mix pharmaceutical prescriptions and fill bottles with prescribed tablets. Prepare and dispense medication. Receive and store incoming supplies and medications. Process records of medication and equipment dispensed to patient.
- Compute charges and enter data in computer, post accounts receivable, accounts payable, and third party payments to computer.
- Trained four Pharmacy Technicians.
- Trusted with confidential information and relied on to make decisions affecting customers' health.

Harrisonville Aquatic Center   **Harrisonville, Missouri**   **Summer 1999 – 2002**

<u>Front Desk Agent</u> (Summer 2001, Summer 2002)
Greeted and registered patrons for use of facility, administered first aid, trusted to balance register and make nightly deposits.

<u>Lifeguard</u> (Summer 1999, Summer 2000)
Monitored activities in swimming areas to prevent accidents and provided assistance to swimmers. Cautioned swimmers in unsafe areas. Rescued swimmers in danger of drowning and administered first aid. Maintained order in swimming areas. Inspected facilities for cleanliness. CPR certified.

Goal oriented

Organization

Innovation and creativity

Attention to details

Leadership

Problem solving

Leadership

ORGANIZATIONS & ACTIVITIES

Sigma Kappa Sorority (Fall 2001 – Present)
    Sophomore Standards, volunteer work
Society for Human Resource Management
    (Fall 2002 – Present)
	Phi Eta Sigma Honorary Fraternity (Spring 2002 – Present)
	    Students exemplifying 3.5 GPA

HONORS & AWARDS

American Royal Metropolitan Scholarship Mechanical Contractors Assoc. Scholarship Presidential Scholarship Semi-Finalist Outstanding Communication Arts Student Award Outstanding Print Journalism Student Award	Harrisonville Teacher's Association Scholarship National Dean's List Who's Who Among America's College & University Students

Jessica Lutz

2829 S. 165 Avenue
Omaha, Nebraska 68130
Phone (402) 123-4567
Jlutz@hotmail.com

November 18, 2006

Mr. Pete Ferraro
Promotion Manager
WSTR c/o Sinclair Broadcasting
2000 West 41st Street
Baltimore, MD 21211

Clearly shows traditional versus T-format

Re: Promotion Writer/Producer position
       advertised on Sinclair Broadcast Group

Dear Mr. Ferraro:

"Knowledge is a process of piling up facts; wisdom lies in their simplification." This quote by Martin H. Fischer sums up the basic premise of what promotion is all about. Whether it's a topical for the 10 o'clock or a new station image campaign, I feel that the heart of a strong Promotions Writer/Producer lies in his/her ability to relate to the audience in ways that truly stick. After reviewing my résumé and tape, you will find that I would be a great asset to WSTR-WB64 as a writer/producer.

Over the last four years I have acquired considerable knowledge of the television industry, particularly in promotions, through my educational experiences. In December I will graduate from Creighton University with a Bachelor of Science in Broadcasting and a minor in Business. The curriculum at this school has benefited me tremendously, mostly due to the hands-on experience I have received on DV cameras, nonlinear editing systems, AP writing, and lighting. On top of the experience with the training, I have studied many of the theories and laws concerning mass media, and I am familiar with many of the industry's trends, such as convergence. Aside from my broadcasting studies, I have kept very active on campus, holding a number of positions in different organizations to help develop leadership and time-management skills. The knowledge and skills I have acquired and the work habits I have developed through my experiences would serve your station well.

To supplement my coursework, I have completed three internships in the Creative Services departments of two different affiliate stations, and I am currently enrolled in a fourth in addition to taking classes in my final semester. These internships have given me additional practice in writing, shooting, and editing pieces and have helped me to conceptualize a project from a blank script to an on-air piece. Over the course of these internships I have become familiar with several different software applications and tape formats, including Avid, Final Cut Pro, Adobe Premiere, DVC-Pro, and Beta. On my résumé tape you will find examples from my past six months as an intern, which were all shot on Beta. At the end of the tape you will find a segment of a long-piece format I researched and wrote for an inductee to the Nebraska Broadcaster's Association Hall of Fame during my first internship.

Mr. Ferraro, the hands-on experience I have received through my internships and coursework has prepared me well for life outside the classroom. I would appreciate the opportunity to discuss my qualifications with you in an interview. I will contact you in two weeks to see if you require any additional information or to answer any questions you may have.

Sincerely,

Jessica Lutz
Enclosure: Résumé, Résumé Tape

Jessica Lutz

2829 S. 165 Avenue
Omaha, Nebraska 68130
Phone (402) 123-4567
Jlutz@hotmail.com

November 18, 2006

Mr. Pete Ferraro
Promotion Manager
WSTR c/o Sinclair Broadcasting
2000 West 41st Street
Baltimore, MD 21211

Re: Promotion Writer/Producer position advertised on Sinclair Broadcast Group

Dear Mr. Ferraro:

"Knowledge is a process of piling up facts; wisdom lies in their simplification." This quote by Martin H. Fischer sums up the basic premise of what promotion is all about. Whether it's a topical for the 10 o'clock or a new station image campaign, I feel that the heart of a strong Promotions Writer/Producer lies in his/her ability to relate to the audience in ways that truly stick. After reviewing my résumé and tape, you will find that I would be a great asset to WSTR-WB64 as a writer/producer.

You seek someone who:	**I have:**
☞ Has real-world experience in promotion writing and producing.	Spent the last six months working in the Promotions and Creative Services Department at an affiliate station in addition to other college coursework. Completed 3 internships.
☞ Has hands-on nonlinear editing experience.	Worked with a variety of nonlinear programs including Avid Xpress, Final Cut Pro and Adobe Premier.
☞ Has strong writing and conceptual skills.	Written and conceptualized pieces for both commercial production and news promotion, including a long-form documentary for Nebraska Broadcasters Association Hall of Fame Inductee Dick Palmquist.
☞ Is an enthusiastic thinker with a great appreciation for on-air promotions.	Focused all four of my internships and related coursework towards working as a Promotions Writer/Producer since my sophomore year of college.

Mr. Ferraro, the hands-on experience I have received through my internships and coursework has prepared me well for life outside the classroom. I would appreciate the opportunity to discuss my qualifications with you in an interview. I will contact you in two weeks to see if you require any additional information or to answer any questions you may have.

Sincerely,

Jessica Lutz
Enclosure: Résumé, Résumé Tape

Present Address:
1831 North Main Street
Sampson, AZ 00369
Phone Number:
117-931-9176

Candice Sprague

Permanent Address:
1396 Maxon Road.
Phoenix, AZ 93111
E-Mail Address:
csprague@yahoo.net

March 23, 2006

Another example of
traditional format versus "T"

Ms. Jamie Grayson
Wells Fargo
3702 Frederick Blvd., Suite 118
Phoenix, AZ 93111

Dear Ms. Grayson:

Initiative and creativity are two qualities that make me a strong candidate for an entry-level position at the Wells Fargo Financial Tucson Branch. As a motivated, team-oriented individual, I would enjoy the opportunity to work with your staff in advancing the goals of Wells Fargo Financial.

As my résumé indicates, I have a grade point average of 3.97 on a 4.0 scale and plan to complete a Bachelor of Science degree in Marketing and Business Management in May 2006. Through completion of various business courses and job opportunities, I have developed a high level of professional experience and business expertise.

Utilizing teamwork, time-management, communication, and operational skills guaranteed the execution of a successful Annual Golf Outing for the Phoenix Area Chamber of Commerce. Effectively managing 30 committee members helped increase revenue obtained from contests and sponsorships, the number of golf participants, and overall profit. Skills enhanced while working for the Phoenix Area Chamber of Commerce will allow me to effectively and efficiently enhance the goals and objectives of Wells Fargo Financial.

Studying abroad in London, England, provided cultural insight and international awareness into the lifestyles and operations of business leaders. Completing an International Business course enhanced my global knowledge through interviews and company tours with the managers of Jaguar, Edward Jones Investments, and the London Underground. These experiences will generate creative insights in progressing Wells Fargo Financial, ensuring that it remains a competitive company that is dedicated to continuously satisfying its customers.

I am confident that my solid combination of work and educational experiences along with my enthusiastic personality matches the qualities you are seeking in an employee. I would appreciate the opportunity to job shadow an employee in an entry-level position to gain insight into the daily operations executed at Wells Fargo Financial. I will contact you mid-April to discuss this opportunity. Thank you for taking the time to review my credentials.

Sincerely,

Candice Sprague

Enclosure: Résumé

Present Address:
1831 North Main Street
Sampson, AZ 00369
117-931-9176

Candice Sprague

Permanent Address:
1396 Maxon Road
Phoenix, AZ 93111
csprague@yahoo.net

March 23, 2006

Ms. Jamie Grayson
Wells Fargo
3702 Frederick Blvd., Suite 118
1020 S 74th Plaza
Phoenix, AZ 93111

Re: Entry-Level Marketing Coordinator

Dear Ms. Grayson:

What type of employee is Wells Fargo looking for? According to your Web site, you need a hardworking, creative individual who has the ability, determination, and motivation to help recruit students at area schools, develop relationships, and coordinate marketing events. I am confident that I fit your criteria and would make a positive impact as the marketing coordinator for your successful company. After exploring the company Web site and reading various news articles, I believe my business expertise and real-world experience make me an ideal match for your company.

You Want An Individual With:	I Have:
♦ Good organizational skills with the ability to handle numerous details	♦ Coordinated the largest fund-raiser for the Chamber of Commerce by organizing the event in its entirety, communicating with over 150 business professionals and implementing more efficient business procedures.
♦ Marketing and sales knowledge	♦ Conducted extensive Marketing Research for the Human Resources Department at Arizona State University.
	♦ Developed a comprehensive Marketing Plan for the company Bee…ing Creative.
	♦ Helped Ladies Workout Express recruit and sign new members through in-depth member benefit explanations.
♦ Excellent interpersonal, verbal communication, and presentation skills	♦ Participated in Jr. Achievement, where I taught 10 business classes to over 35 fifth-grade students.
	♦ Served as a Peer Advisor and led discussions and taught 10 classes for 15 freshman students.
♦ A strong work ethic	♦ Earned a 3.97/4.0 grade point average toward a Bachelor of Science degree with a double major in Business Management and Marketing.
♦ International exposure	♦ Developed cultural insight and international awareness while studying International Business abroad in London, England.
	♦ Participated in company tours with managers of Jaguar, Edward Jones, and the London Underground.

As my résumé indicates, my solid educational background and professional business experience will help Wells Fargo continue to provide services for individuals, schools, and businesses worldwide. I am confident that my ingenuity, ambition, and focus along with my enthusiastic, outgoing personality match the qualities you are seeking in a Marketing Coordinator. I will call your office in mid-April to answer any questions you may have concerning my qualifications. Thank you for your time.

Sincerely,

Candice Sprague
Enclosure: Résumé

PART THREE

Thank-You Notes

Creating a Personalized Thank-You Note

When do I need to send a thank-you note?

You should send a handwritten, personalized thank-you note to express your gratitude while searching for a job. You should always send one (or more if you interviewed with more than one individual) after a personal interview or referral to another hiring professional. This includes an informational or mock interview or an extended conversation at a job fair if you won't be sending your cover letter and résumé until later.

Can I just e-mail the message?

Because e-mail and instant messaging replace our traditional "snail mail," a handwritten and personalized message will take on even more importance. E-mail messages can be crafted and sent in a matter of minutes; but it takes more thought to purchase a card, handwrite a message, and mail a written note. This extra effort pays off. Although an e-mail may be appreciated, it will probably be quickly deleted; your handwritten message is likely to remain on the reader's desk to be glanced at several times. If time is critical (you suspect they will make a decision within one day) or you know the receiver prefers to handle his or her correspondence through e-mail, it is acceptable to send your message through e-mail.

The extra effort that goes into sending a handwritten message may provide a real advantage over other applicants. Purchase your cards and stamps ahead of time so that you'll be able to send the card within 24 hours of your interview. The cards should be fairly plain (white with silver or gold type works well), but you can add a little of your personality by using an ink stamp with your school logo (I use a green paw print) or another subtle distinction.

What if my handwriting is sloppy?

Take your time to put together a neatly written document. Your printing or handwriting size should be readable and uniform throughout the card. Unless you have extra cards, you should always put your draft together on a separate sheet of paper and make sure it will fit in the space available. You can print rather than write in cursive if you need to. Don't resort to using smaller lettering toward the bottom of the card because you are running out of space.

Is it *always* appropriate to handwrite these notes?

Usually, there are two exceptions. The first is if the employer has indicated he or she prefers to handle all correspondence electronically. Even if you do send an e-mail thank you, the message still needs to be individualized and sent directly to each person to whom you owe gratitude. Choose at least one element of your message that speaks directly to the reader rather than sending the same message to more than one person.

The other exception is if the organization's culture and tone of the interview was quite formal. If this is the case, use a standard business letter for a thank you. There are instances when a more formal, typed thank-you letter is appropriate. Typically, this is done when you have more than one letter to write and can use the Microsoft Word mail merge function, or, as mentioned before, when the business operates on a more formal basis. Because these are typed letters, it is important to sign each letter to add a personal touch. Several sample thank-you notes addressing a variety of situations follow.

145

March 12, 2006

Dear Dr. Lim,

Thank you for selecting my application and spending time interviewing me for Drake's Presidential Scholarship.

I am excited about the honors courses and premed major your university offers and welcome the opportunity to set high academic standards in the classroom. If selected for this honor, I pledge to work diligently to achieve academic excellence at your university.

Once again, I appreciate all the time and energy you put forth to encourage academic excellence at Drake. Your effort to help students select a career path that is right for them is commendable.

Sincerely,
Jeremy Peak

July 11, 2006

Dear Ms. Frerking,

Thank you for taking time out of your busy schedule to participate in a mock interview with me today.

Your insight and candid feedback definitely helped improve my interviewing skills. I also genuinely appreciate the information you offered regarding the financial field. As I pursue a career in the banking industry, your tips will be kept in mind.

Thanks for sharing your knowledge and expertise. CU students are lucky to have such helpful employers willing to participate in our annual mock interview program.

Sincerely,
Jessica Moore

April 7, 2006

Dear Mr. Parker,

Thank you for taking time out of your busy schedule to interview me for your recruiter position.

After spending time at your headquarters, I am more convinced than ever that Cerner is Kansas City's premier employer. Recruiting exceptional talent to help you meet your goal of expansion into the European market would be a rewarding experience.

I look forward to meeting the rest of your department in the near future.

Sincerely,
Ridge Yount

P.S. - I'll keep my fingers crossed that your son's high school football team wins the playoffs this weekend.

January 2, 2006

Dear Sara,

Thank you for encouraging me to call your friend Kevin to discuss employment opportunities at LMP.

We had a delightful conversation this afternoon, and I look forward to meeting the rest of his team. My skills appear to be well in line with their unique needs.

Thanks for having such confidence in my ability. Having friends like you in my court definitely will make the job search a more enjoyable experience. I hope to be in a position to help you in some manner in the near future.

Grateful for your help,
Lane Hermelink

August 11, 2006

Dear Ms. Bewley,

I enjoyed meeting you and learning about your new and improved Hallmark Web site. Thank you for spending so much time discussing your vision for future changes.

While reflecting on the interview I thought of another example in which I've demonstrated leadership and creativity. Two years ago I initiated a fund-raising effort to support a youth basketball team. Working with a team of three, we successfully raised $2,500 organizing a 3-on-3 tournament for local middle school students.

I look forward to offering my enthusiasm and creative energy to Hallmark.

Sincerely,
Allison Gerdts

P.S. After I returned home from the interview, my mom showed me a card I'd made for her when I was ten. On the back I'd included the borrowed slogan "when you care enough to send the best."

February 7, 2006

Mr. Matthew Adkins
Director of Human Resources
KMF Auditing Firm
1001 Grand Ave.
Kansas City, MO 60014

Mr. Adkins:

Thank you for the opportunity to meet and interview with you today. The values and goals of KMF Auditing seem to fit perfectly with my beliefs. The Assistant Auditor position sounds challenging and exciting.

KMF Auditing's involvement in the community should be commended. You are making Kansas City a better place to both work and raise a family. I was very impressed by all that you do and look forward to becoming involved in such a program!

Again, I appreciate the time you took from your busy schedule to meet with me. If you have any further questions, please feel free to contact me. I look forward to hearing from you soon.

Sincerely,

Davis Platt

Action Verbs

Management/Leadership Skill

achieved	consolidated	executed	lobbied	rejected
administered	contracted	generated	managed	reorganized
affected	controlled	governed	merged	replaced
analyzed	coordinated	handled	motivated	reported
appointed	decided	headed	officiated	restored
approved	delegated	hired	organized	reviewed
assigned	deliberated	hosted	oriented	scheduled
attained	developed	implemented	originated	spearheaded
authorized	directed	improved	outlined	staffed
bought	disputed	incorporated	overhauled	strategized
chaired	eliminated	increased	oversaw	strengthened
channeled	emphasized	initiated	planned	supervised
chose	encouraged	inspected	presided	terminated
commanded	enforced	inspired	prioritized	united
commended	enhanced	instituted	produced	
conceived	established	launched	recommended	
considered	evaluated	led	reevaluated	

Communication/People Skills

addressed	confronted	enlisted	mapped	recruited
advertised	consulted	explained	marketed	referred
approached	contacted	expressed	mediated	reinforced
arbitrated	conveyed	formulated	met	renegotiated
arranged	convinced	furnished	met with	reported
articulated	corresponded	greeted	moderated	researched
authored	counseled	incorporated	motivated	resolved
bargained	cultivated	influenced	negotiated	responded
bonded	debated	interacted	observed	reunited
briefed	defined	interfaced	opposed	solicited
broached	described	interpreted	outlined	specified
called	developed	interviewed	participated	spoke
clarified	directed	involved	persuaded	suggested
collaborated	disclosed	issued	presented	summarized
communicated	discussed	joined	promoted	synthesized
composed	drafted	judged	proposed	translated
condensed	edited	lectured	publicized	wrote
conferred	elicited	listened	reconciled	

Research Skills

accumulated	correlated	found	linked	researched
acquired	critiqued	gathered	located	reviewed
analyzed	detected	grouped	measured	searched
benchmarked	determined	identified	noted	solved
canvassed	diagnosed	illuminated	noticed	studied
chartered	discovered	indexed	organized	summarized
checked	disproved	inquired	pinpointed	surveyed
cited	documented	inspected	polled	systematized
clarified	evaluated	interpreted	probed	tested
collected	examined	interviewed	profiled	uncovered
compared	experimented	invented	proved	wrote
conceived	explored	inventoried	rated	
concluded	extracted	investigated	related	
conducted	formulated	isolated	reported	

Helping Skills

acclimated	clarified	encouraged	harmonized	referred
accommodated	coached	engaged	helped	rehabilitated
accompanied	collaborated	enlisted	inspired	represented
adapted	connected	ensured	insured	resolved
advised	contributed	exchanged	intervened	secured
advocated	cooperated	exercised	invited	simplified
aided	coordinated	expedited	maintained	supported
answered	counseled	facilitated	modified	treated
appreciated	dealt	familiarized	motivated	undertook
arranged	demonstrated	favored	offered	unified
assessed	devoted	fostered	performed	upheld
assisted	diagnosed	furthered	presented	volunteered
brought	eased	granted	provided	welcomed
cared for	educated	guided	recovered	

Organization

activated	controlled	incorporated	prepared	screened
altered	corresponded	inspected	processed	set up
approved	decentralized	inventoried	proofread	specified
arranged	described	listed	provided	standardized
assembled	dispatched	logged	published	streamlined
booked	distributed	maintained	purchased	structured
catalogued	edited	monitored	recorded	submitted
categorized	estimated	moved	reduced	supplied
centralized	executed	observed	registered	systematized
charted	filed	obtained	reserved	tabulated
circulated	finalized	opened	responded	updated
classified	formalized	operated	restructured	validated
closed	formulated	orchestrated	retrieved	verified
coded	gathered	ordered	reviewed	
collected	generated	organized	routed	
compiled	implemented	overhauled	scheduled	

Creative Skills

acted	crafted	fashioned	merchandised	refined
adapted	created	formed	modeled	revised
amended	customized	formulated	modified	revitalized
applied	designed	founded	molded	rewrote
began	developed	illustrated	originated	shaped
brainstormed	directed	improvised	perceived	solved
combined	dispensed	initiated	performed	staged
composed	displayed	instituted	photographed	synchronized
conceived	drew	integrated	planned	updated
conceptualized	entertained	introduced	presented	visualized
condensed	established	invented	produced	
constructed	evaluated	loaded	redesigned	

Technical Skills

adapted	converted	extrapolated	overhauled	solved
assembled	debugged	fabricated	preserved	specialized
authored	designed	fortified	printed	standardized
automated	determined	graphed	programmed	studied
built	developed	inspected	rectified	trained
calculated	devised	installed	regulated	upgraded
co-authored	diagrammed	maintained	remodeled	utilized
computed	dissected	mapped	repaired	weighed
conserved	engineered	navigated	replaced	
constructed	exposed	operated	restored	

Financial/Data Skills

accounted	budgeted	developed	invested	projected
added	calculated	discounted	keyed	quantified
adjusted	compared	disputed	liquidated	quoted
administered	computed	diversified	managed	reconciled
allocated	conserved	enumerated	marketed	reduced
analyzed	corrected	equaled	measured	reevaluated
anticipated	counted	estimated	netted	researched
appraised	cut	excluded	paid	retrieved
assessed	decreased	exempted	planned	sold
audited	depreciated	figured	priced	speculated
automated	detailed	financed	procured	tallied
balanced	determined	forecasted	programmed	

Training Skills				Transferable Skills
adapted	developed	initiated	showed	achieved
advised	enabled	instilled	simulated	attained
affiliated	encouraged	instructed	stimulated	attended
announced	endorsed	keynoted	taught	developed
asked	evaluated	lectured	tested	employed
captured	exhibited	mentored	trained	encountered
clarified	explained	motivated	transmitted	enhanced
coached	facilitated	narrated	tutored	entered
communicated	fielded	nurtured	updated	familiarize
conducted	focused	officiated		fine-tuned
coordinated	graded	oriented		mastered
critiqued	guided	persuaded		observed
defined	individualized	presented		obtained
delivered	informed	set goals		perfected
				refined
				strengthened

Accomplishments

accelerated	concentrated	fulfilled	picked	saved
accomplished	contributed	gained	piloted	selected
achieved	created	graduated	pioneered	served
added	decreased	induced	prevented	shortened
advanced	designated	initiated	progressed	spearheaded
amplified	discovered	inspired	prompted	spurred
aspired	distinguished	instigated	pursued	stabilized
assumed	doubled	instituted	qualified	streamlined
attracted	earned	introduced	raised	strengthened
awarded	effected	invented	ranked	surpassed
beat	elected	invited	reaped	tightened
bolstered	eliminated	maximized	rebuilt	transformed
boosted	enacted	minimized	recognized	trimmed
broadened	ended	modernized	redesigned	tripled
capitalized	enlarged	motivated	reduced	undertook
caused	enriched	moved	resulted	updated vitalized
challenged	established	multiplied	revamped	vitalized
championed	exceeded	named	reversed	widened
changed	excelled	nominated	reworde	won
cofounded	expanded	orchestrated	safeguarded	
completed	founded	overhauled	salvaged	

Résumé Checklist

Please check of the following items as you evaluate your résumé.

Did you use an Objective or Profile targeted to the opening, occupation, or field based on the employer's needs? (i.e., To obtain the human resource internship at Hallmark during Summer 2006).

Are Keywords from job opening, occupation, or field incorporated into your résumé? If the job asks for teamwork skills, you have clearly shown that you have developed your teamwork skills somewhere in your résumé, perhaps in a profile (summary of skills), job, or campus involvement. Review keyword guides for sections relevant to your area.

Does your education section quickly identify your background?

- Clearly identifies your degree, major and minor, when you will graduate, and where you went to school.

- Lists relevant coursework (in a logical order) if you aren't close to graduation (unless work experience or campus involvement is more impressive).

- Discusses GPA, hours worked, or percent financed as is relevant to your situation.

- Highlights major course activities if your work experience section is weak or if you need filler (e.g., Conducted marketing research project for the City of Maryville with a group of three students).

Do your Work and Leadership Experience sections make the best of the experience you have to offer?

- Descriptions clearly identify what you did at a position unless a job is completely self explanatory such as Dog Walker.

- Action verbs are used to describe all positions; you have varied the action verbs used.

- Internships are clearly labeled.

- Irrelevant, long-ago jobs are eliminated or grouped together in a Work History or Other Work Experience section.

- All jobs have a title, organization, location, and dates listed.

- Use present tense for present situations and past tense for past jobs and experiences.

- Use active descriptions "Managed" and avoid passive constructions such as "Was responsible for managing".

- You have eliminated statements such as "Duties included".

Have you included at least one Accomplishment or Transferable Skill for each position?

- Emphasis is on skills and accomplishments, not just responsibilities.
  (Skill ex: Obtained the ability to handle pressure and work in a team.)
  (Accomplishment Ex: Consistently received positive evaluations from superiors and co-workers.)

Have you used concrete examples whenever possible?

- Quantify - use numbers, percentages, or dollar amounts (e.g., Organized events for groups of 20–30).
- Qualify any statement you can (e.g., Trusted by Academic Dean to uphold confidentiality).

Is your résumé completely error-free?

- Have you included enough words? (e.g., Check your word count and compare it to samples similar to yours).
- Did you run it through grammar and spell check?
- Have you read it out loud word-by-word?
- Have you asked a friend and professional to review the document?

Does your résumé look *highly* professional?

- Overall appearance makes an excellent first impression (passes the 12-inch test).
- Name and contact information is formatted in a manner so that your name is prominent.
- Professional e-mail address is included without hyperlink.
- At least two fonts were used in the document—Font type and size are easy to read. My favorite is Times New Roman for Headings (12 or 13) and Arial for body (9.5 or 10).
- All bullets and lines are highly professional (don't use * or – as a bullet).
- Section headings clearly separate sections and identify the material in their section; section headings and words that follow are separated with adequate white space.
- Formatting within sections is uniform and consistent (spacing, font size, bullets, slashes, numbers, dates, punctuation).
- Layout on the page utilizes paper space appropriately (not too much or too little white space).
- You only have one space after periods.
- Margins on sides are equal (fold the paper in half to test this).
- Underlining, italics, and bolding are appropriately used.
- Key information is easy to find.
- Professional 24 lb. bond 100 percent cotton white or off-white résumé paper and laser printing are used.
- No typos – spelling and grammar is perfect.
- No use of "I", "me", or "my"; minimized use of articles (a, an, the).
- Length appropriate for your level of education and experience (usually one page).
- Critical information is listed at the beginning with less important details listed toward the bottom.
- Most college students' sections will follow this order: Objective and/or Profile, Education, Work Experience, Leadership or Organizations, Honors/Achievements (You may not have *all* of these sections).
- A statement regarding references being available upon request is only used to balance page; using "Portfolio available upon request" is okay.